i

Collected Masonic Papers

2014 Transactions
of the
Louisiana Lodge of Research

Collected Masonic Papers

2014 Transactions of the
Louisiana Lodge of Research

MW. Clayton J. Borne, III, 33°, PGM
Worshipful Master
W. Michael R. Poll, PM
Secretary

Published by the Louisiana Lodge of Research
by agreement with
Cornerstone Book Publishers
Copyright as a collection © 2014 by Louisiana Lodge of Research
http://louisianalodgeofresearch.org

Cornerstone Book Publishers
New Orleans, LA
www.cornerstonepublishers.com

ISBN:1613422385
ISBN-13:978-1-61342-238-0

MADE IN THE USA

Table of Contents

Past Masters of the Louisiana Lodge of Research

1989-90: William J. Mollere
1991: Ballard L. Smith
1992: Irving I. Berglass
1993: Philip J. Walker, Jr
1994: Beryl C. Franklin
1995: Ernest C. Belmont, Jr
1996: Thomas P. Brown
1997: Larry H. Moore
1998: Darrell L. Aldridge
1999: Edward W. Brabham, Jr
2000: Howard F. Entwistle, Jr
2001: Johnnie K. Hill
2002: Richard L. James
2003: Terrell Howes
2004: Glenn Cupit
2005: Robert Bazzell
2006: John Bellanger
2007: Jimmy Leger
2008: Ion Lazar
2009: Bill Richards
2010: Ricks Bowles
2011-14: Clayton J. Borne, III

The Grand Lodge of Louisiana, F&AM
P.O. Box 12357
5746 Masonic Drive
Alexandria, Louisiana. 71315-2357
Website: http://www.la-mason.com

M:W: Earl J. "Mickey" Durand
Grand Master
R:W: William J. Mollere
Deputy Grand Master
R:W: Will P. Gray
Grand Senior Warden
R:W: Guy Jenkins
Grand Junior Warden
M:W: Woody Bilyeu, PGM
Grand Treasurer
M:W: Roy B. Tuck, Jr., P.G.M.
Grand Secretary

Collected Masonic Papers

Communication and Masonic Membership
by Charles H. Penn, III, P.G.M.
The Grand Lodge of Louisiana

Some fourteen million years ago, our apelike ancestors left the shelter of the jungles of eastern Africa to make their way on its vast plains. These human beings had to compete for survival against thousands of lions, leopards, rhinoceroses, cape buffaloes, and other predators. A lion or leopard can run faster than a human being; the rhinoceros has a tougher hide; the buffalo is mean-tempered and, in addition, has vicious horns. As food, smaller animals that might serve as such can climb trees, while others are quite fleet-footed.

No visitor surveying that primeval scene could have predicted that thin-skinned, defenseless, prehistoric man-creatures would not only survive but multiply and ultimately become earth's dominant animals. That they did so was because they had:

A brain that could solve problems instead of reacting by instinct and could remember what worked in the fight for survival and what didn't.

An upright posture that freed the hands. The human hand with its opposed thumb gradually became a precise instrument for making weapons, starting fire, cooking in vessels, fashioning clothing, and storing food.

And also because:

The art of communication makes it possible to hunt in pairs or in small groups. Directions can be shouted, refined, or relayed; objects can be given names. And classified as fast or slow, safe or dangerous, edible or inedible. Not only words but facial expressions and gestures can be utilized. Events can be recalled, analyzed, discussed, and lessons learned that can be used in the future.

Communication makes teamwork and group effort possible. You can teach a reasonably smart baboon to stack three boxes on top of each other to facilitate reaching a stallk of bananas. But to teach three baboons to build a stack of three boxes is a far more difficult task. In any problem whose solution must be wrought by group effort, communication is absolutely essential.

If you were to ask a human resources officer of almost any major corporation what he deemed to be the most important asset a management-level employment candidate could possess, the answer would almost certainly be: **communications skills.**

Realizing the importance of communication to every phase of society, why then, does the Masonic fraternity hold that importance in almost total disregard when attempting to address what many perceive as the organization's foremost modern-day problem: the rapid decline of its membership numbers?

If and when Freemasonry finally decides to move forward in a unified group effort to bring that problem to solution, communication must play not only a vital role, but a role that must be determined as indispensable. Communication must be utilized in every area of this endeavor, but for purposes of discussion we will focus upon three broad fronts.

    1) Communication between Masonry and the general public
    2) Communication between Masonic leadership and the Craft at
       large
    3) Communication between Symbolic and Appendant bodies

Communication between Masonry and the general public

Public perception of Freemasonry is in a pitiful state and in many quarters the fraternity is largely unknown to the general public on any basis at all. Simply put, Masonic organizations have become islands unto themselves, turned inward, and have lost appreciation and recognition in the non-Masonic world. Masonry's reluctance to be actively involved in our communities and its lack of willingness to communicate with good men about the fraternity are the chief reasons for Masonry's inability to bring new initiates to its altars.

There are many stories of Masonry's history of public service and it is this type of service that has helped make our fraternity so strong in the past. For some time now, we have gone into our Lodge rooms and boasted to one another of our self-pride in being Freemasons and of what Masonry has done for us. We have boasted to each other concerning the founding of our country by Freemasons. We have told and retold ourselves about all the famous men who were members of our noble Craft. But in all this, we are preaching to the proverbial choir who sing in a church far removed from the mainstream of everyday modern life.

Over the years Freemasonry in this country has developed in directions many no longer consider vital to society. Yes, our many charitable organizations do give us some positive public exposure, but they do very little to communicate what our fraternity is or what it does. The Shrine Hospital network is far and away Masonry' greatest philanthropic institution as judged by public perception, but very few people outside the organization have any idea that every Shriner is a Freemason.

Specifically, what can we do? If we are to regain the lofty status we once held, we must become a recognizable part of the public. Our real civic responsibility is to convince the world by our actions that we are Masons. We should do those things which provide leadership in improving the physical, moral, and emotional status of our environment. In fact, we should communicate by our actions the kind of public image which the whole world can admire and will wish to emulate. The time is long overdue when societies like ours must come into the open with a public declaration of aims so all men may see that even in the cloud of present day social confusion, there is one organization with strong and worthy ideals. We must plan an organized effort to seek out the good men of our communities and tell them what Freemasonry stands for and what it does.

We need to communicate the idea that we are interested in them because of their quality as men and if they seek membership, they will be welcomed. Failure to communicate these things to the public can only contribute to our current membership decline.

Communication between Masonic leadership and the Craft at large

If Freemasonry is to halt or perhaps even reverse its current membership trend, it must demand for itself strong and vibrant leadership. Not too many years ago our rolls were swelled with members and dues income was more than sufficient to provide for the organization's needs. Elected Masonic leaders, especially on the Grand Lodge level, were able to enjoy leading the several fraternal bodies simply by carrying out time-honored traditions. Unfortunately, for today's leader, that luxury no longer exists. During the past fifty or so years, because of relative inactivity, we have become weak and have shrunken in size. We desperately need to revitalize ourselves. If anyone believes we can improve our lot by continuing to do as we have always done in the past, he is sadly mistaken.

Today's Masonic leaders must set the Craft to labor as never before. It is imperative for those leaders to immediately and thoroughly inform all Masons as to the severity of the problems facing the institution. Feedback from the rank and file must be earnestly solicited as a means of establishing two-way communication (Not top-down, but truly reciprocal). That feedback must then be evaluated to ascertain whether the members really do care about those problems and what thoughts and suggestions might be brought forth to effect solutions. If those solutions predicate changes in our way of doing business, then the vast majority must be willing to move forward for progress, working shoulder to shoulder without divisiveness, lest we fail from internal strife.

We must contact and reestablish communication with our inactive, demitted, and NPD members who, for some reason, have lost interest in our fraternity. We must make every effort to contact our "lost" degree candidates and ascertain their reason for "dropping out". We must somehow rekindle that spark of interest that first brought them to a Masonic altar. I strongly suspect that one of the reasons for Masonic membership decline is the lack of interest by Brethren and/or candidates who feel that the fraternity has little to offer them. In some cases this is rightly justified. Freemasonry has evolved, to a large extent, into a social club with some philanthropic interests and has failed to respond to the real interests and desires of its members. The sad result of this neglect on the part of leadership is that no matter how many new initiates we bring into the fold, their number doesn't begin to approach that of those who leave by demit or NPD. Unfortunately, this exodus has occurred rather silently without any communicative effort on our part to ascertain the real reason.

In order to stymie this problem, we must give the Brethren something of value. We must establish programs that engage them and encourage their participation, thus revitalizing their productivity. By creating an environment in which the program is based upon the wants and needs of the Brethren, the leadership becomes instrumental in generating needed changes. But here again, communication plays a key role. The members must be asked to declare their ideas and wishes. Then, armed with that knowledge, an achievable program can be designed that is both appropriate to the situation and satisfying to the membership.

Communication between Symbolic, Appendant, and Collateral bodies

Our comments concerning the appendant Masonic bodies will be rather brief. We do feel, however, that a few observations appertaining thereto should be incorporated here.

For many years, perhaps for far too long, have the appendant and collateral bodies ridden upon the broad back of Symbolic Masonry with very little effort expended in the reciprocal return of service. Admittedly, many Brethren who have chosen to dedicate the majority of their Masonic labors to the appendant bodies are still active in their "Blue" Lodges, but that, at best, is no better than a fifty-fifty proposition. For far too long have our "Blue" Lodges been left alone to fend for themselves, all the while serving as the "factory" for appendant body membership.

The time is long overdue for appendant Masonry to return to the pronounced opinion that the Symbolic Lodge is the chief cornerstone of the entire Masonic institution and unquestionably its supreme organization rather than viewing it as just an "entry-level induction center" for the other bodies. All Masonic organizations must come together in a unified effort, pooling talent and assets to market and promote Freemasonry.

In *Morals and Dogma*, Pike tells us: "Masonry is action and not inertness. It requires its initiates to work, actively and earnestly, for the benefit of their brethren, their country, and mankind. It is the patron of the oppressed, as it is the comforter and consoler of the unfortunate and wretched. [...] It is the advocate of the common people in those things which concern the best interest of mankind. [...] Its fidelity to its mission will be accurately evidenced by the extent of the efforts it employs, and the means it sets to foot, to improve the people at large and to better their condidtion."

In order to preserve our Craft and to carry it on to future generations as a positive vital force, we, as American Masons, need to make immediate and dramatic changes in our way of doing business, not in the Craft's philosophy and ritual, but in the way we practice that ritual. We must develop both an internal and an external understanding of that Masonic philosophy through enhanced communication.

"Aurum nostrum non est aurum vulgi"
by J. Quincy Gotte

"That God is good and merciful, and loves and sympathizes with the creatures He has made;...that all men are our brothers, whose wants we are to supply, their errors to pardon, their opinions to tolerate, their injuries to forgive; that man has an immortal soul, a free will, a right to freedom of thought and action; that all men are equal in God's sight; that we best serve God by humility, meekness, gentleness, kindness, and other virtues which the lowly can practice as well as the lofty; this is the new Law, the Word..."

Albert Pike's – *Morals and Dogma*

The Degrees of the AASR are designed to inculcate within its members a sense of obligation towards our fellow man. It doesn't fly the banner of any particular country or religion above another, but encourages the patriotism and faith of its members towards their respective governments and religions in respect towards benevolence. Its practices are founded upon all of the great common and profound virtues of many different philosophies and religions from across this magnificent global sphere upon which we live. The practicing member is the life of the Craft; the protector and barer of the Light that shines the Wisdom of the Grand Architect, which prevails by way of Charity, Truth, Hope, and Tolerance.

As Scottish Rite Masons we are to constantly be at labor within ourselves, practicing a "Spiritual Alchemy" transforming something common into something special. "Aurum nostrum non est aurum vulgi" (our gold is not the common gold) is the thought to ponder within the heart of every Scottish Rite Mason. Gold is a precious metal, but is most precious when it has passed through the fires of refinement.

The Degrees of our Craft teach us the importance and relevance of trials. We are taught of the vast purification process that trials are intended to accomplish within our own individual lives as well as the lives of others around us. We find that trials are not only for strengthening Faith, but for building Hope, for perfecting Charity, and for clarifying Truth. Faith, Hope, Charity, and Truth should be forged through Tolerance; they should not be regarded as separate jewels, but as an absolute whole, and a work towards perfection. So much of the concept of Charity has been directed to tangible or monetary provisions, and although this type of giving requires Faith that the process will make a difference and the Hope for brighter days, we may tend to fall short on the importance of Tolerance within our work.

Faith and Hope is the result of a spiritual experience sought after in Truth within an individual, and is made tangible through the outward act of Charity. But there is a lower and a higher degree of Charity.

As we travel through this physical realm, we naturally and rightfully place value on the tangible forms of Charity, because it is relevant and it produces an almost immediate positive effect within ourselves and on our society. We must also realize that a great portion of Charity relies on Tolerance, and that it is exhausting to be charitable without it. We all experience from time to time, that numbing cold wind of judgment that blows from the north through our minds when a higher degree of our Tolerance is required of us. Whether it is of spiritual, economic, political, or ethical concern, as Scottish Rite Masons, we have obligated ourselves to encourage the building of character, and to live a noble and honorable life by reflecting the Light of our Creator, Blessed be He. We learn through our Degrees that knowledge obtained and not put to use is vain, and that we must work diligently with what we are given towards the good of humanity. Therefore, when our Charity is forged through Tolerance, we are practicing our Charity in a higher degree. When I say higher and lower, it is with the understanding that neither degree of charity is more valuable than the other, but the two together are complete as it has been refined through the fires of our Spiritual Alchemy.

A Look Back at Louisiana Masonic History
Michael R. Poll, P.M.
Secretary, Louisiana Lodge of Research

If we think of the word "light" to mean understanding or knowledge, then we do not have much light concerning many aspects of early Louisiana Masonry. We are not completely sure of what rituals were used by the lodges, the nature and composition of the lodges, the attitude of the Grand Lodge or many other aspects that would give us a clear picture of the times and events. Even when we do understand *what* happened, it is often unclear as to *why* it happened. One cause for the lack of understanding of our early days is the long absence of so many of the pre-1850 Proceedings (and other documents) of the Grand Lodge and other bodies. Effort has been made in recent years to locate and preserve many of the valuable old Proceedings and documents, but still many of the important ones remain missing. In addition, effort has been made to piece together many small aspects of our history so that they can be put together into larger pictures (maybe by future generations) to help us better understand the times.

In Spring of 2014, with the kind assistance of Glenys Waldman and Cathy Giaimo of the Masonic Library & Museum of Pennsylvania, I was able to secure a photocopy of an interesting small documents titled "Extracts from the Records of the Grand Lodge of Louisiana, Ancient York Masons (Sitting of the 16th of May, 1812)." The document is reproduced following this introduction. I don't know if this is, as it says, only "extracts" from the complete Proceedings or if this is actually what the new Grand Lodge of Louisiana published for its first Proceedings. In any event, it provides fascinating reading and provides us with important information about the first Grand Lodge session.

Following the "Extracts" is a chart of some Louisiana presiding officers from 1811-1855 (the controversial years) that was gathered by using old Grand Lodge Proceedings, the 1822-47 Minutes Book of the Grand Consistory of Louisiana (long considered lost) as well as other documents, charts and publications from the Grand Lodge and Supreme Council of Louisiana. The goal is to try and understand who the players were at the times of some of the important events in Louisiana Freemasonry. Sadly, available records do not provide a complete record of all names.

The presiding officers are listed for the following Louisiana bodies of which I was able to located records (in order of creation): The Grand Consistory of Louisiana (1811 creation - *note*: from 1813 to 1832 known as the Grand *Council* of Louisiana); the Grand Lodge of Louisiana (1812 creation); the Supreme Council of Louisiana (1839 creation); The Louisiana Grand Lodge (1847 creation); The Consistory of New Orleans (1852 creation).

✓

EXTRACTS from the Records of the GRAND
LODGE OF LOUISIANA, Ancient York-Masons.

(Sitting of the 16th of May, 1812.)

WHEREAS, at a Grand Communication of Ancient
York-Masons, held in the City of New-Orleans, State
of Louisiana, at the Lodge room of the Worshipful
Lodge *La Parfaite Union*, No. 29, situated in the
Suburb St. Mary, corner of Camp and Gravier streets,
on the 15th day of May, in the year of our Lord 1812,
and of Masonry 5812.

" It was unanimously *resolved* " that the Worship-
" ful Master of the W. Lodge *La Parfaite Union*,
" No. 29, the Senior of the Regular Lodges of this
" State, be requested to issue his Summons to the
" Masters, Past-Masters and Officers of the several
" ancient and regularly constituted Lodges in this State,
" to meet in Convention, to take into consideration the
" interests of the true Craft, and to deliberate on the
" necessity of establishing a GRAND LODGE in this
" State ".

(Sitting of the 13th of June, 1812.)

Whereas, at a Grand Convention of Ancient York-
Masons, held in the City of New-Orleans, State of
Louisiana, in the Lodge room of the W. Lodge *La
Parfaite Union*, No. 29, situated in the Suburb St.
Mary, corner of Camp and Gravier Streets, on saturday,
the 13th of June, in the year of our Lord 1812, and of
Masonry 5812.

PRESENTS

First, The Worshipful Master, Past-Masters and
Officers of the Worshipful Lodge *La Parfaite Union*,
No. 29, regularly constituted by the Right-Worshipful
GRAND LODGE of South Carolina, by Warrant bearing
date the 21th of November, 1793.

(2)

2d. The Worshipful Master, Past-Masters & Officers of the Worshipful Lodge *La Charité*, No. 93, regularly constituted by the Right Worshipful GRAND LODGE of Pennsylvania, by Warrant bearing date the 1st of March, 1802.

3d. The Worshipful Master, Past-Masters & Officers of the Worshipful Lodge *La Concorde*, No. 117, regularly constituted by the Right Worshipful GRAND LODGE of Pennsylvania, by Warrant bearing date the 29th of October, 1810.

4th. The Worshipful Master, Past-Masters & Officers of the Worshipful Lodge *La Persévérance*, No. 118, regularly constituted by the Right Worshipful GRAND LODGE of Pennsylvania, by Warrant bearing date the 27th of October, 1810.

5th. The Worshipful Master, Past-Masters, & Officers of the Worshipful Lodge *L'Etoile Polaire*, No. 129, regularly constituted by the Right Worshipful GRAND LODGE of Pennsylvania, by Warrant bearing date the 3d of June, 1811.

The Grand Convention having met agreably to Summons issued by the W. Brother P. F. DUBOURG, present Master of the W. Lodge *La Parfaite Union*, No. 29, for the express purpose to take into consideration the interests of the true Craft, and to determine whether it wou'd be advantageous to establish a Grand Lodge in the State of Louisiana.

The following motion was made and seconded, viz: That saturday next, the 20th of June, be the day appointed for the election of the Grand Master, the Deputy Grand Master and other Grand Officers, to form a Grand Lodge for the State of Louisiana, free and independent of all other Masonick Jurisdiction, under the style and title of Grand Lodge of Louisiana, ancient York-Masons. The said motion was, *Nemine contradicente*, agreed to.

(3)

(Sitting of the 20th June, 1812.)

And Whereas, at a Grand Convention of Ancient York-Masons, held on the 20th June 1812, and of Masonry 5812, at the Lodge room of the Worshipful Lodge *La Parfaite Union*, No. 29, situated as above, being the day appointed for the election of a Grand Master, Deputy Grand Master and other Grand Officers, to form a Grand Lodge for the State of Louisiana, free and independent from all other masonick jurisdiction, under the Title and Denomination of GRAND LODGE OF LOUISIANA, Ancient York-Masons.

The Convention proceeded by ballot to the election of the aforesaid Grand Officers, and on casting up the votes, it appeared that the Right Worshipful Brethren, herein after named, obtained a majority, and were duly elected to the dignities of the Grand Lodge, to wit :

The Worshipful P. F. DUBOURG, present Master of the Worshipful Lodge *La parfaite-Union*, No. 29, GRAND MASTER.

The Honorable and Worshipful L. C. MOREAU LISLET, Past-Master, & Member of the Worshipful Lodge *L'Etoile Polaire*, No. 129, DEPUTY GRAND MASTER.

The Worshipful Jean BLANQUE, present Master of the Worshipful Lodge *La Charité*, No. 93, SENIOR GRAND WARDEN.

The Worshipful François PERNOT, present Master of the Worshipful Lodge *La Concorde*, No. 117, JUNIOR GRAND WARDEN.

The Worshipful J. B. PINTA, present Master of the Worshipful Lodge *La Persévérance*, No. 118, GRAND TREASURER.

J. B. VERON, present Senior Warden of the W. Lodge *la Persévérance*, n° 118, GRAND SECRETARY.

(4)

The Worshipful Mathurin PACAUD, Past-Master and Member of the Worshipful Lodge *L'Étoile Polaire*, No. 129, GRAND ORATOR.

Yves LEMONNIER, present Junior Warden of the W. Lodge *La Charité*, No. 93, GRAND PURSUIVANT.

Augustin MACARTY, present Junior Warden of the W. Lodge *La Parfaite Union*, No. 29, GRAND STEWARD.

In the same sitting, the Right Worshipful GRAND MASTER was duly & regularly installed, proclaimed, saluted and congratulated, agreably to ancient form and usage.

It was moreover unanimously *resolved* by the Grand Convention, that the R. W. Grand Master should be authorised to install the other Grand Officers elected, and to designate a convenient day for their installation, and the opening of the Grand Lodge.

(Sitting of the 11th *July,* 1812.

And Whereas, saturday, the 11th day of July, in the year of our Lord 1812, and of Masonry 5812, having been fixed upon by the R. W. Grand Master for the Installation of the Grand Officers, and for the opening of the Grand Lodge.

The Members of the Grand Lodge of Louisiana, met agreably to the Summons, to them directed by the R. W. Grand Master, in New-Orleans, at the Lodge room of the Worshipful Lodge *La Parfaite Union*, situated as aforesaid, and the R. W. Grand Master proceeded to the Installation of the Grand Officers elected, according to the order of their respective dignities, and the said Grand Officers were duly proclaimed, saluted and congratulated agreably to ancient form and usage, of which proceedings appear more fully on the Records of the Grand Convention and of the Grand Lodge.

Seton

Date	1811	1812	1813
Commander in Chief Grand Consistory of Louisiana	?	?	Emanuel Gigaud
Grand Master Grand Lodge of Louisiana	*	Pierre Francois DuBourg	Pierre Francois DuBourg
Grand Commander Supreme Council of Louisiana	*	*	*
Grand Master Louisiana Grand Lodge	*	*	*
Commander in Chief New Orleans/ Charleston Consistory	*	*	*

Date	1814	1815	1816
Commander in Chief Grand Consistory of Louisiana	Emanuel Gigaud	Jean Pinard	Jean Pinard
Grand Master Grand Lodge of Louisiana	Pierre Francois DuBourg	Jean Soulie	Jean Soulie
Grand Commander Supreme Council of Louisiana	*	*	*
Grand Master Louisiana Grand Lodge	*	*	*
Commander in Chief New Orleans/ Charleston Consistory	*	*	*

Date	1817	1818	1819
Commander in Chief Grand Consistory of Louisiana	Jean Pinard	Jean Pinard	Jean Pinard
Grand Master Grand Lodge of Louisiana	Jean Soulie	J. Moreau Lislet	J.B. Modest Lefebvre
Grand Commander Supreme Council of Louisiana	*	*	*
Grand Master Louisiana Grand Lodge	*	*	*
Commander in Chief New Orleans/ Charleston Consistory	*	*	*

Date	1820	1821	1822
Commander in Chief Grand Consistory of Louisiana	Jean Pinard	J.B. Modest Lefebvre	J. Moreau Lislet
Grand Master Grand Lodge of Louisiana	Yves Le Monnier	Aug. Macarty	J. F. Canonge
Grand Commander Supreme Council of Louisiana	*	*	*
Grand Master Louisiana Grand Lodge	*	*	*
Commander in Chief New Orleans/ Charleston Consistory	*	*	*

16

Date	1823	1824	1825
Commander in Chief Grand Consistory of Louisiana	J. Moreau Lislet	J. Moreau Lislet	J. Moreau Lislet
Grand Master Grand Lodge of Louisiana	D. F. Burthe	J. F. Canonge	John Henry Holland
Grand Commander Supreme Council of Louisiana	*	*	*
Grand Master Louisiana Grand Lodge	*	*	*
Commander in Chief New Orleans/ Charleston Consistory	*	*	*

Date	1826	1827	1828
Commander in Chief Grand Consistory of Louisiana	John Henry Holland	John Henry Holland	John Henry Holland
Grand Master Grand Lodge of Louisiana	John Henry Holland	John Henry Holland	John Henry Holland
Grand Commander Supreme Council of Louisiana	*	*	*
Grand Master Louisiana Grand Lodge	*	*	*
Commander in Chief New Orleans/ Charleston Consistory	*	*	*

Date	1829	1830	1831
Commander in Chief Grand Consistory of Louisiana	John Henry Holland	John Henry Holland	John Henry Holland
Grand Master Grand Lodge of Louisiana	J.F. Canonge	John Henry Holland	John Henry Holland
Grand Commander Supreme Council of Louisiana	*	*	*
Grand Master Louisiana Grand Lodge	*	*	*
Commander in Chief New Orleans/ Charleston Consistory	*	*	*

Date	1832	1833	1834
Commander in Chief Grand Consistory of Louisiana	John Henry Holland	Auguste Douce	Auguste Douce
Grand Master Grand Lodge of Louisiana	John Henry Holland	John Henry Holland	John Henry Holland
Grand Commander Supreme Council of Louisiana	*	*	*
Grand Master Louisiana Grand Lodge	*	*	*
Commander in Chief New Orleans/ Charleston Consistory	*	*	*

Date	1835	1836	1837
Commander in Chief Grand Consistory of Louisiana	**A.W. Pichot**	**Pierre Soule**	**Pierre Soule**
Grand Master Grand Lodge of Louisiana	**John Henry Holland**	**L. H. Ferrand**	**L. H. Ferrand**
Grand Commander Supreme Council of Louisiana	*	*	*
Grand Master Louisiana Grand Lodge	*	*	*
Commander in Chief New Orleans/ Charleston Consistory	*	*	*

Date	1838	1839	1840
Commander in Chief Grand Consistory of Louisiana	**L. H. Ferrand**	**A. W. Pichot**	**A. W. Pichot**
Grand Master Grand Lodge of Louisiana	**John Henry Holland**	**John Henry Holland**	**A. W. Pichot**
Grand Commander Supreme Council of Louisiana	*	**Orazio de Attellis, Marquis de Santangelo**	**Orazio de Attellis, Marquis de Santangelo**
Grand Master Louisiana Grand Lodge	*	*	*
Commander in Chief New Orleans/ Charleston Consistory	*	*	*

Date	1841	1842	1843
Commander in Chief Grand Consistory of Louisiana	A.W. Pichot	A.W. Pichot	J. F. Canonge
Grand Master Grand Lodge of Louisiana	A.W. Pichot	Jean Lamothe	E. A. Canon
Grand Commander Supreme Council of Louisiana	Orazio de Attellis, Marquis de Santangelo	Jean Jacques Conte	Jean Jacques Conte
Grand Master Louisiana Grand Lodge	*	*	*
Commander in Chief New Orleans/ Charleston Consistory	*	*	*

Date	1844	1845	1846
Commander in Chief Grand Consistory of Louisiana	J. F. Canonge	J. F. Canonge	G. A. Montmain
Grand Master Grand Lodge of Louisiana	E. A. Canon	Robert J. L. de Preaux	Felix Gracia
Grand Commander Supreme Council of Louisiana	Jean Jacques Conte	J. F. Canonge	J. F. Canonge
Grand Master Louisiana Grand Lodge	*	*	*
Commander in Chief New Orleans/ Charleston Consistory	*	*	*

20

Date	1847	1848	1849
Commander in Chief Grand Consistory of Louisiana	Robert J. L. de Preaux	Robert J. L. de Preaux	Robert J. L. de Preaux
Grand Master Grand Lodge of Louisiana	Felix Gracia	Felix Gracia	Lucien Hermann
Grand Commander Supreme Council of Louisiana	J. F. Canonge	James Foulhouze	James Foulhouze
Grand Master Louisiana Grand Lodge	*	*	John Gedge
Commander in Chief New Orleans/ Charleston Consistory	*	*	*

Date	1850	1851	1852
Commander in Chief Grand Consistory of Louisiana	?	?	?
Grand Master Grand Lodge of Louisiana	Lucien Hermann	John Gedge	H. R. W. Hill
Grand Commander Supreme Council of Louisiana	James Foulhouze	James Foulhouze	James Foulhouze
Grand Master Louisiana Grand Lodge	John Gedge	*	*
Commander in Chief New Orleans/ Charleston Consistory	*	*	John Gedge

21

Date	1853	1854	1855
Commander in Chief Grand Consistory of Louisiana	?	?	Claude Pierre Samory
Grand Master Grand Lodge of Louisiana	H. R. W. Hill	William M. Perkins	William M. Perkins
Grand Commander Supreme Council of Louisiana	James Foulhouze	Charles Claiborne	Charles Claiborne
Grand Master Louisiana Grand Lodge	*	*	*
Commander in Chief New Orleans/ Charleston Consistory	John Gedge	?	?

Date	1856	1857	1858
Commander in Chief Grand Consistory of Louisiana	Claude Pierre Samory	Albert Pike	Albert Pike
Grand Master Grand Lodge of Louisiana	William M. Perkins	William M. Perkins	Amos Adams
Grand Commander Supreme Council of Louisiana	J. J. E. Massicot	James Foulhouze	James Foulhouze
Grand Master Louisiana Grand Lodge	*	*	*
Commander in Chief New Orleans/ Charleston Consistory	*	*	*

The Four Hirams of Tyre
by A.S. MacBride, Scotland
The Builder April, 1917

INTRODUCTION

It will, no doubt, surprise many Masons, as well as non-Masons, to be told that there are four Hirams of Tyre mentioned in the scripture narrative of the building of King Solomon's Temple of Jerusalem. Recently the Revd. Br. Morris Rosenbaum, P. P. G. Chaplain, Northumberland; Hollier-Hebrew Scholar, University of London; called the attention of the Masonic fraternity to the views of Meir Lob Malbim, the famous Rabbi of Kempen, as shown in his Commentary on the books of Kings and Chronicles. The learned Rabbi maintains, that these books refer to two Hirams who were employed at the building of the Temple, and that many passages in these books are only reconcilable on that supposition. While considering this proposition and searching for information regarding it, some interesting indications became apparent, leading to the conclusion, that there are two Kings of Tyre, as well as two Artisans of Tyre, mentioned in the sacred narrative; and all called by the name of Hiram. Following up these indications and reviewing the whole subject, at full length, this article on "The Four Hirams of Tyre" is the result.

Let us then consider the two propositions indicated, viz : First, that in the narration of the building of King Solomon's Temple at Jerusalem, as given in the books of Kings and of Chronicles, two kings of Tyre, called Hiram, are mentioned. Second, that in the narration above referred to, two artisans of Tyre, called Hiram, are also mentioned.

I. THE TWO KINGS CALLED HIRAM

The first mention in the Bible of the name of Hiram is in II Samuel V. 2, where we read: "And Hiram of Tyre sent messengers to David, and cedar trees, and carpenters, and masons, and they built David an house." Referring to the same circumstance, we read in I Chronicles XIV. 1: "Now, Hiram king of Tyre sent messengers to David, and timber of cedars, and masons, and carpenters, to build him an house." In I Kings V. 1 we are informed: "And Hiram king of Tyre sent his servants unto Solomon; (for he had heard that they had anointed him

king in the room of his father:) for Hiram was ever a lover of David."
In II Chronicles 11. 3, it is recorded: "And Solomon sent to Hiram the
king of Tyre, saying, as thou didst deal with David my father, and
didst send him cedars to build him an house to dwell therein, even so
deal with me." After the Temple had been built, as we learn from I
Kings IX. 10: "It came to pass at the end of twenty years, when
Solomon had built the two houses, the house of the Lord, and the
King's house, . . that then king Solomon gave Hiram twenty cities in
the land of Galilee. And Hiram came out from Tyre to see the cities
which Solomon had given him; and they pleased him not. And he
said: What cities are these which thou hast given me, my brother?
And he called them the land of Cabul unto this day." (This word
"Cabul" expresses contempt. According to Josephus, it means, "that
which does not please.")

Let us try to arrange the circumstances here mentioned in
chronological order. From II Samuel V. 5, and I Kings II. 11, we learn
that David reigned thirtythree years in Jerusalem. It was in the early
years of his reign there, that David received from Hiram, cedar trees,
masons and carpenters to build his house. This was, in all probability,
thirty years before the death of David and the crowning of Solomon.
In the fourth year of Solomon's reign the building of the Temple was
begun and Hiram, king of Tyre, sent his servants to assist in the work.
Twenty years afterwards, Solomon gave Hiram, twenty cities in the
land of Galilee. Such is an outline of the events connected with Hiram
king of Tyre, as related in the Hebrew scriptures, and if we closely
examine them the question will naturally arise: was the Hiram who
sent cedar-trees, and masons and carpenters to David the Hiram of
the twenty cities? If so, then when Solomon gave him the twenty
cities, he must have reigned in Tyre for fifty-four or more, years; an
almost incredulous length of reign in those days in the east. (This
figure is arrived at as follows: from the building of King David's house
to the crowning of King Solomon, 30 years: from the latter event to
the beginning of the building of the Temple, 4 years: from the
beginning of the Temple to the giving of the twenty cities, 20 years:
In all 54 years.)

Considering the conditions of royal government prevalent in the
eastern world in the days of Solomon and David, we are surely entitled

to assume that Hiram would be at least twenty years of age when he sent his carpenters and masons to build a house for David his friend. If this is right, Hiram must have been at least seventy-four years old when he "came out from Tyre to see the cities which Solomon had given him." For an aged eastern monarch to undertake a journey through a rough and barren country, such as Galilee, seems not at all natural. One can hardly suppose, also, that after his long intimacy with David and Solomon he would be without a fairly accurate knowledge of the cities adjacent to his own kingdom, and that he would have needed to undergo the toil of such a journey in order to know what they were like. This journey indicates more the curiosity of an active, young, monarch, than the careful action of one approaching, if not actually the octogenarian stage. The phrase, also, in Kings V. I: "for Hiram was ever a lover of David," scarcely accords with the idea of an old friend. It seems more to indicate a youthful admirer whose father, or near relative, had long been a friend of David.

The only known source of information on this subject, outside of the Hebrew scriptures, are the two Hellenistic historians: Menander of Ephesus, and Dius; the latter being largely dependent on the former. The statements of these historians have been preserved by the Jewish writer Josephus, and from these we learn that Hiram I, son of Abi-baal, reigned in Tyre from 970 to 936 B. C. and that the building of Solomon's Temple dates from the eleventh year of Hiram. If this is correct, he could not be the Hiram who sent masons and carpenters to build an house to David, according to the sacred narrative, at least thirty-four years before the building of the Temple. If Hiram, son of Abi-baal, was the first of the name, then who was the Hiram of David's house referred to in II Samuel, V. 2? This difficulty is explained by some writers, by suggesting that Abi-baal was a distinctive, or honorary name; and that his proper name was Hiram: and this, according to Kitto's Cyclopedia, "is rendered probable by the fact that other persons of the name of Hiram occur in the series of kings of Tyre." On the whole, taking everything into account, the natural and probable conclusion seems unavoidable, viz: that the Hiram of the building of David's house and the Hiram of the twenty cities were two distinct persons. If we assume that they were one and the same, we are faced with the following improbabilities.

(1) That David must have built his house shortly before his death, after reigning in Jerusalem for about thirty years; which does not agree with the sacred narrative.

(2) That his intrigue with Bethsheba, the mother of Solomon, must also have occurred in his old age, which is not quite likely.

(3) That the various campaigns, detailed in the narrative, after the building of his house, must also have taken place in his advanced years, viz: the Philistine war at Baal-perazim, and the war in the valley of Rephaim; the conquests of Moab, of Zobah, of Syria, of Edom and of Ammon; the revolt of Absolom, various insurrections, another Philistine war, in which David waxed faint in battle; and the battles of Gob and Gath, et cetera.

(4) That Solomon must have been a child when he was crowned king of Israel, and when he began to build the Temple; also, when he married Pharaoh's daughter, and gave his famous judgment in the case of the two women who claimed each to be the mother of the same child; and further, when he had established a fame for wisdom and learning that had spread over many lands; all of which is very improbable.

Reading the Hebrew scriptures in a common sense way, there seems no reasonable doubt that none of these improbabilities occurred. David built his house previous to the Bethsheba incident, and the various wars referred to. Wars were protracted and trying in his day, and we can scarcely imagine those mentioned as being carried on by an old monarch of seventy years, nor in less than twelve to fifteen years. Add to this the intervals of peace, in which the Ark was taken to Zion, and in which preparations were made for the building of the Temple, the three years of famine, and other things mentioned in the sacred narrative; and we may safely say that, at least, thirty years intervened between the building of David's house and his death.

In contrast to this contradictory and unsatisfactory theory, that there is only one Hiram, king of Tyre referred to, in the sacred history of the building of the Temple; the assumption that two kings of Tyre, called Hiram are therein mentioned, at once solves our doubts and difficulties, and makes the narrative plain and natural.

The course of events seems to have been as follows: David of Israel and Hiram of Tyre were great friends and, probably, about the same age. After David captured Jerusalem, his friend in Tyre sent him masons and carpenters to build an house for him. War had for years devasted Judea, causing the arts and manufactures to be neglected. The peaceful occupations of the builder and the artist had been abandoned for that of the warrior, and hence David had to obtain those from Tyre; which was then famous all the world over for its arts and manufactures. Time passed and age began to steal over the hardy shepherd, warrior and poet king. Twenty-six years after the building of his house his friend Hiram dies, and is succeeded by his son Hiram; and, seven years afterwards, David himself is gathered to his fathers and Solomon, then thirty years of age, ascended the throne. In the fourth year of his reign Solomon began to build the Temple, with the assistance of Hiram, king of Tyre, the successor of Hiram the friend of David. In furtherance of this view of the subject we find in the letter sent by Hiram to Solomon, agreeing to the request for assistance in the building of the Temple, the following words: "And now I have sent a cunning man, endued with understanding of Huram my fathers." Here we have, surely in the light of common sense, a clear indication that the predecessor of Hiram on the Tyrian throne was also called Hiram.

Reviewing all the circumstances as related in the sacred narrative, and taking into account the testimony of Menander that the building of the Temple was begun in the eleventh year of the reign of Hiram; there appears only one conclusion open to us, viz: that the Hiram who sent masons and carpenters to build a house for David, and the Hiram who, fifty-four years after that event, refused the twenty cities offered to him by king Solomon; were not the same but were both kings of Tyre; of the same name, and, probably, father and son.

II. THE TWO *ARTISANS CALLED HIRAM

IN the traditions of Masonry connected with the M. M. degree, the central figure is that of "Hiram Abif." A martyr to fidelity and honour, his memory has been held sacred by the Craft. Yet, historically, there is very little known of him. By many, if not by the most, of those who troubled themselves to think on the subject, the traditions regarding him, until recently, were considered to be mythological legends similar to those on which the ancient mysteries were formed, and altogether devoid of truth. The fact that in the Biblical accounts of the building of King Solomon's Temple there is no mention, nor apparently the smallest hint, of his death, has been accepted as a proof that he did not die, during the building of that structure. Dr. Oliver, the well known Masonic writer, evidently considered the tradition of his death as mythical, for in the "Freemason's Treasury," Lecture XLV, he says: "It is well known that the celebrated artist was living at Tyre many years after the Temple was completed."

But let us examine the Biblical narrative a little more closely than we have hitherto done. Assuming for the time being as correct, the generally accepted belief that only one artisan of the name of Hiram, or Huram, is mentioned in that historical account of the building of the Temple; we are immediately confronted with three contradictions demanding attention. These are:

(1) in the descriptions of his parentage;

(2) in the descriptions of his qualifications;

(3) in the periods named of his arrival at the Temple.

In the first place then, let us look at

THE DESCRIPTIONS OF HIRAM'S PARENTAGE

In 2 Chron. H. 14, Hiram is said to be: "the son of a woman of the daughters of Dan." In I Kings VII. 14, he is described as: "the Son of a widow woman of the tribe of Naphtali." Now, no man can have two mothers, and no mother can belong to two tribes. On what supposition then, can these two differing descriptions be reconciled? Is it some mistake as to the tribe to which the mother belonged? With writers unacquainted with the tribes of Israel, or of the peculiarities of Hebrew history, that might be. But the writers of the books of Kings and Chronicles had an intimate knowledge of all these things, and we can scarcely suppose for a moment any such mistake.

The tribe of Dan occupied the hilly country in the immediate neighborhood of the Philistines and Samson the celebrated warrior and patriot was of that tribe.

* The word "Artisan" is here used in its proper sense as one skilled in Art; a master of Arts.

Unable to subdue the Philistines the Danites, after the death of Samson, migrated to the plains of the upper Jordan around the city of Laish, which was then the granary of Sidon. Their proximity to Tyre, no doubt, resulted in intermarriages with the Tyrians; and hence, there would be nothing very remarkable in "the Son of a woman of the daughters of Dan," being a famous artisan of Tyre.

The tribe of Naphtali were located in the mountains on the northern border of Palestine; and from their nearness to Tyre and the necessities of trade from the sea-coast, they had regular intercourse with the Tyrians, and intermarriage would, consequently, more or less result. Thus there seems nothing extraordinary in the recorded fact, that a Tyrian artisan was "the son of a widow woman of the tribe of Naphtali."

There is little likelihood that, in either of these two cases, the writer of the book of Kings, or the writer of the book of Chronicles, would make any mistake in the matter of lineage; for on this point the Hebrew writers seem to have been very particular. The fact that in both instances the father is not mentioned, adds weight to the correctness of the description of the mother; and, if there was only one artisan of the name of Hiram at the building of the Temple, we have before us the insuperable difficulty of believing that he had two mothers.

Let us now pass on to consider, in the second place;

THE DESCRIPTIONS OF HIRAM'S QUALIFICATIONS

In 2nd. Chronicles II. 14, Hiram is described as: "Skillful to work in gold, and in silver, in brass, in iron, in stone, and in timber, in purple, in blue, and in fine linen, and in crimson; and also to grave any manner of graving, and to find out every device." In 1st Kings VII. 14, he is called: "A worker in brass, and he was filled with wisdom and understanding, and cunning to work all works in brass." Now, just think for a little on these two descriptions. The one is skillful to work metals—gold, silver, brass and iron; also stone and timber. In weaving and in dyeing, in engraving and in every device, he is an expert. He is an all around architect—a marvel, a genius, a man of large experience and, no doubt, of ripe years, whose fame would be sure to go down the ages. The other is merely a worker in brass—no doubt a man of good parts, but limited in experience and knowledge— probably young in years, and, according to the description, as yet only a worker in brass. This statement that his craftsmanship is confined to brass is most carefully noted by the historian, for it is reiterated in the description. He says: "A worker in brass filled with wisdom and understanding, and cunning to work all works in brass," He repeats the words "in brass," as if he was afraid that the individual he was describing might be mistaken for some other person of the same name, also celebrated as an artisan and a worker, at the building of the Temple.

Considering these two descriptions, is it reasonable to believe that they refer to the same individual? They are not loose, nor in any way vague. On the contrary, they are very precise and detailed, and no one reading them, without prejudice, would imagine them to refer to the same artisan.

We now come to our third point, viz:

THE PERIODS NAMED OF HIRAM'S ARRIVAL AT THE TEMPLE

In 2nd Chronicles II. 13, before the work of the Temple was begun, Hiram king of Tyre in his letter to Solomon says: "And now I have sent a cunning man endued with understanding," etc. In I Kings VII. 13, after the house of the Lord and the house of Solomon had been built, we are informed: "King Solomon sent and fetched Hiram out of Tyre." In the one statement we are told that before the house was built a skillful man was sent to King Solomon by Hiram King of Tyre; in the other that after the house was built Solomon "sent and fetched" Hiram out of Tyre. These periods were twenty years apart; for the house of the Lord took seven years, and the house of Solomon and the courts of the Temple other thirteen years in building.

To understand the biblical narrative properly one has to keep in view that there are several "finishes" mentioned, and that these refer only to certain parts of the work at the building of the Temple. The first "finish" is mentioned in I. Kings VI. 9: " So he built the house and finished it"—that is the mason-work, or shell of the building. Then comes the second part of the work, consisting of the carpenter-work of the roof, and of the chambers around about, as stated in verses 9 and 10; and in verse 14, the narrative goes on to say: "So Solomon built the house and finished it." The third part of the work described, consists of the decorations—the gold plating and gilding. Verse 22 says: "And the whole house he overlaid with gold, until he had finished all the house." The fourth part of the work is stated to have been the internal fittings and carvings of the house, and the building of the inner court, and the whole is summed up in verse 38, as follows: "And in the eleventh year, in the month of Bul, which is the eight month, was the house finished throughout all the parts thereof, and according to all the fashion of it. So was he seven years in building it."

So far as we have followed the narrative, the house itself, in its plan and embellishments, has been finished; but the Temple is still far from being completed. The outer courts and the houses of the king, with all their magnificence and ornamentation; the pillars of the porch, and the altars and utensils of the inner court, have not yet been begun. These were to take other thirteen years to construct and finish. In the meantime, let us go on. The house of the forest of Lebanon, the porch of judgment, Solomon's Palace, the palace for Pharaoh's daughter, and the great court; had all just been built when the sacred narrative is abruptly interrupted by the statement: "And king Solomon sent and fetched Hiram out of Tyre." All the work of building proper had been completed, but many things had yet to be done before the sacrifices and magnificent services of the Hebrew religion could be begun and maintained at the Temple. But, if Hiram was sent by the king of Tyre before the work was begun, why did Solomon, at this particular stage, need to send and "fetch" him out of Tyre ? Had he gone back to Tyre after some years of laborious work, and was he again needed to complete the building? There are one or two objections to the idea. If he did return to Tyre, we would naturally expect the historian to give us some indication of his having done so. But, search as we may, there is not the smallest hint, or indication of that. All writers on the subject, differing as they do on many points, agree that Hiram had the superintendence of the work at the building of the Temple. Is it likely then, that he could have gone back, while the work was unfinished? The time necessary for such a journey in those days would have so interfered with the progress of the building operations that we are scarcely entitled to assume such a thing, unless on something approaching substantial grounds. The custom then, and for many centuries afterwards, with artisans such as Hiram, was to make their home for the time being wherever their work was. Building operations in connection with temples were necessarily of long duration. In the present case they had probably already stretched over fifteen years. The building of the holy house had occupied seven years, and the royal houses and the courts were finished, so far as mason and carpenter work were concerned; and, as they occupied thirteen years to complete, we may safely estimate that at least eight of these thirteen years had already passed when "Solomon sent and fetched Hiram out of Tyre." In all probability then, Hiram had already spent thirteen years in Jerusalem and, if alive, was still there. If that was so, why and wherefore did Solomon need to send and fetch him out of Tyre? So far as all the records go, the periods named of Hiram's arrival at the Temple are not consistent with the course of events, and are contradictory to each other; so long as we assume there was only one Hiram engaged at the work of the Temple.

These three contradictions as to the Parentage, Qualifications, and Period of arrival at the Temple, which we have now been considering, must apparently remain inexplicable, unless on the natural and, at present, the only reasonable explanation that there were two artisans of the same name, engaged at the work of that famous structure. This hypothesis reconciles those contradictions, makes clear the biblical narrative, explains certain hitherto unintelligible statements, and lends corroborative testimony to the truth, in its substance, of the Masonic tradition of the death of Hiram Abif. In the light of this hypothesis let us now review the whole circumstances mentioned in the sacred narrative.

The first Hiram is "the son of a woman of the daughters of Dan," and arrives at the beginning of the building of the Temple. He is an all around artisan, skillful to work in stone, timber, gold, iron, etc. He superintends the building operations. It is a task of no common difficulty. A great Temple has to be built on the top of a rugged hill, almost entirely surrounded by sharp precipices. Immense walls, the lowest of which is to be 450 feet high, have to be reared up in the valley out from the precipices, and the intervening space has to be filled up with earth in order to make room for the Temple with all its courts and palaces on the top. This work has to be done under the peculiar conditions that neither hammer, nor axe, nor any tool of iron is to be heard in the main structure, that is the sanctuary; while it is being built. All this would require great skill, knowledge and experience. Stonework, timber-work, and metal-work of various kinds have to be executed. The Sanctuary has to be covered inside and outside with gold. Great curtains, with cherubims and other devices, have to be manufactured. Carvings on stone, and on timber; engravings on gold and silver; have to be done, and done in the highest and most skillful manner possible. The work is not only stupendous in its nature; it is also magnificent in its character. Well, the years pass on and, at the seventh, the house of the Lord and the inner court have been built. Then began the work of the outer courts and the royal palaces. These, while parts of the Temple scheme, were not considered as parts of the sanctuary, and hence, sacred silence was no longer a necessary condition. All was now bustle. The sounds of hammer and chisel, and the stir of toil filled the air, while the great courts and palaces were gradually erected. Other eight years passed in this work, and Hiram the first, with his wonderful genius and skill, built a structure whose fame has been echoed down through the long corridors of Time. Now it is at this stage that Hiram the first disappeared and Hiram the second, "the son of a widow woman of the tribe of Naphtali" came into view. Everything, except the molten brass-work, has been done. Why did Hiram the first not do it? That he was perfectly capable, there can be no reasonable doubt. Why then, did Solomon need to send for Hiram the second to do it? It is evident that Hiram the first was no longer available. Why? Neither scripture narrative nor profane history, so far as we can trace, give any answer to this question. But the traditions of Masonry supply a very clear and natural answer. Hiram the first was dead, and hence Solomon sent and fetched Hiram (the second) out of Tyre, to finish the work. Everything had been completed except the brass-work. and Hiram the second is described specially as "a worker in brass." Five more years passed and the final finish of the Temple came. The mighty brass pillars—the casting of which was a wonderful achievement—the various altars and utensils, the golden candlesticks etc., were all made and put in their places and, with full pomp and sacrifice, Solomon dedicated and consecrated the house of the Lord.

In this way, on the assumption that there were two Hirams engaged at the work of the Temple the sacred narrative is clear and coherent; and the seeming inconsistencies and contradictions we have referred to, disappear.

But there still remain one or two passages in the narrative which puzzle us. In I. Kings VII. 45, we read: "And the pots and the shovels and the basins, and all these vessels, which Hiram made to king Solomon for the house of the Lord, were of bright brass." In II. Chronicles IV. 16, after ascribing as in the book of Kings, the various things made by Hiram—the pillars, the bases, the layers, and the sea with twelve oxen under it—we read: "And the pots also, and the shovels, and the flesh-hooks and all their instruments, did Hiram, his father make to king Solomon, for the house of the Lord, of bright brass." Here we have evidently a parenthetical remark interjected by the writer of the narrative with the object of making plain to the reader some fact which would be otherwise obscure. The words "of bright brass" arrest our attention. What do they mean? They evidently want to emphasize that the pots, shovels, and all the work of brass done by "Hiram, his father" were of bright brass that is, malleable brass; while the pillars, the bases, the lavers, as mentioned in the context were of cast brass. This distinction is associated with the words "his father." Whose father could it be, but the father of the person whose work is being described ? In verse II of the last mentioned chapter in

Chronicles, we read: "And Huram made the pots and the shovels and the basins. And Huram finished the work that he was to make for King Solomon for the house of God." Now, according to Hebrew scholars the words here translated "Huram" in both instances, are distinct, and different in the original. In I. Kings VII. 40, our translation should read: "And Chirom made the layers and the shovels and the basins. So Chiram made an end of doing all the work, etc.": and in II. Chronicles IV. 11, it should read: "And Chiram finished the work that he was to make for king Solomon" etc.

In view of the distinction in the names, and of the apparent parenthetical character of the 45th verse in I. Kings VII. and of the 16th verse in II. Chronicles IV., the reading of the sacred narrative appears to be as follows, beginning at I. Kings VII. 40:

"But Chirom made the lavers and the shovels and the basins, and Chiram made an end of the work that Chirom was to have made king Solomon for the house of the Lord: the two pillars, and the two bowls of the chapiters that were on the top of the two pillars; and the two net-works, to cover the two bowls of the chapiters which were upon the top of the pillars; and four hundred pomegranates for the two net-works, even two rows of pomegranates for one net-work, to cover the two bowls of the chapiters that were upon the pillars; and the ten bases, and ten lavers on the bases; and one sea, and twelve oxen under the sea:—but the pots and the shovels, and the basins; and all those vessels which Chirom made to king Solomon for the house of the Lord were of bright brass."

In the same way beginning at II. Chronicles IV. 11, we would read: "But Churam made the pots, and the shovels, and the basins; and Chiram finished the work which Churam was to have made for king Solomon for the house of God—to-wit: the two pillars, and the pommels, and the chapiters which were on the top of the two pillars, and the two wreaths to cover the two pommels of the chapiters which were upon the pillars. He made also bases, and lavers made he upon the bases: One sea and twelve oxen under it; But the pots, and the shovels and the flesh-hooks, and all the instruments which Churam, his father, did make to king Solomon for the house of the Lord were of bright brass."

This reading of the narrative, seems to us, the only one that gives any appearance of consistency and plain sense. The repetition of the name "Hiram" in I. Kings VII. 40, and its use in verse 45; the repetition of "Huram" in II. Chronicles IV. 11, and the words "Huram his father" are all inexplicable and confusing, as they stand. The explanation that makes everything plain and clear is that Hiram the son made the pillars, the lavers, etc., of cast-brass, and that Huram his father made the pots, basins, etc., of bright or malleable brass. In this view the words "his father" (in the original "Abif") is rendered quite natural and intelligible, and accords with Masonic tradition.

In all the variations of the Masonic traditions, the Hiram whose death occurred immediately preceding the completion of the Temple is named "Hiram Abif." This designation becomes significant only in view of the fact that another Hiram, his son, also superintended at the building of the Temple and finished the work which his father would no doubt have finished had he lived a few years longer. Why should the designation "Abif" have been given if there was no other Hiram engaged at the Temple? It surely. indicates not only another Hiram, but also that the other was the son of the Hiram so named.

The Hiram whom Solomon "fetched out of Tyre" is described as the son of a widow. This description accords exactly with the theory now advanced. If Hiram Abif was dead and his wife alive, his son Hiram would naturally be the son of a widow.

The expression "sent and fetched" is peculiar and is also perhaps very significant. It seems to indicate in all probability that the King Solomon sent an escort for Hiram. Our Rev. Brother Rosenbaum thinks this was to protect him from his father's enemies. With this we can scarcely agree. These enemies were all too insignificant to demand for him a royal escort. Ordinary guards as was usual for travelers, would have been sufficient so far as safety was concerned. A royal escort was, and is a mark of honour and it seems much more probable that this respect was shown to the son, in honour of the fame and memory of the father.

This theory of the two Hirams-Artisans at the building of the Temple also harmonizes with the statement made by Dr. Oliver to which reference has already been made, viz: "It is well known that the celebrated artist was living in Tyre many years after the Temple was completed." This statement has been used as an argument against the truth of the Masonic tradition regarding the death of Hiram. But if there were two Hirams the statement of Dr. Oliver and the tradition of Hiram's death may both be true. Hiram the son may very probably have returned to Tyre and lived, let us fondly believe, many years the worthy son of a noble father.

My Ideal Masonic Lodge
by Raymond Sean Walters
Presented to the Ohio Lodge of Research Sept. 13, 2014

It was first suggested to me several years ago that I should consider writing a book about my experiences and travels as a Freemason. From then until now, I have actually been uncertain what exactly I should write a book about. I have written a number of papers and even presented them, but to write a book sounds pretty involved. This will be another attempt at a written paper, and since this one is based on personal thoughts and opinions, I will give it a go.

I was first informed by W Bro. Chad Simpson that the subject of this paper should be my thoughts as to what would be the ideal masonic lodge — a paper that affords any writer to offer opinions based on their own thoughts, perspectives, and personal understanding. I found the idea to be so drastically different that I agreed to consider writing a paper and submitting it.

My Masonic journey has been filled with a considerable amount of personal anguish, though I will readily admit that I have met a number of Freemasons that seem to have gained some understanding of Freemasonry's teachings and have become better at applying those teachings to their own daily living. Those Freemasons have helped me by teaching me or showing me a different perspective on many things, helping to keep me in due bounds by reminding me to use the tools of my craft, or any other tools at my disposal.

Freemasonry and the lessons it conveys are NOT rocket science. If the stated purpose of taking a good man and showing him how to become a better man are taken at face value, then becoming that better man should be an attainable objective for all who enter Freemasonry's doors. One such reminder is that

Freemasonry is a system of morality, veiled in allegory and illustrated by symbols. It has become apparent to me after 24 years of travel as a Freemason, that the lessons taught as well as lessons learned are not apparent to all claiming the title Freemason. If the lessons are readily apparent, it must be the application thereof that becomes the challenge for some.

I will begin with the qualification requirements of one seeking admission to our order. I will be referencing a ritual called More Light, written by H.W. Sanders. The More Light ritual parallels another ritual called Ecce Orienti, which is a coded version of the exposure by H.W. Sanders.

A candidate is asked a series of questions about qualifications to become a member and if it is of his own volition that he seek to be admitted into the lodge and order. The same candidate is conducted through his ceremony of initiation, with no member present expecting him to actually remember the lessons and symbolism taught during the ceremony.

This same process is repeated until the candidate is eventually pronounced a Master Mason and in many cases having only had to learn what could be considered rudimentary lessons to be deemed proficient. It is now that the application of those lessons is expected, and required.

With this being said, my first question is, and always has been was the candidate actually taught? It is stressed during these ceremonies that the candidate be instructed and proves himself as all brothers and fellows who have gone this way before him. Has he proven himself? If so, how?

My ideal here would be that the candidate actually be taught lessons of substance, not just lessons of ritual. Teach him lessons that may cause him to re-think all that he knew in the outside world prior to coming into the oblong-square. If Freemasonry is to be a transformation, transforming requires work. Work can be physical or intellectual — but it is work that is required.

This work should begin in the EA degree, and no candidate should be simply passed through without being given a true education — lessons that will impact his thinking, and guide him toward making a transformation within him first, thereby enabling him to effect positive change in the outside world he must live, work and even struggle in on a daily basis.

It is an especial duty of the lodge as a whole to TEACH and shouldn't fall to only one particular instructor that the Master may have assigned. Learning experience can often be better through a series of lectures and lessons with more than one instructor, so that over time many things can be learned, and later applied.

My second ideal situation for any lodge is that what I have indicated makes for a good candidate was hopefully applied previously to all the brothers and fellows who had gone before him. Training and preparation is required before advancement in any field of endeavor, and should be as equally important in this speculative science we have freely obligated ourselves to work and study at.

Even though one may be titled an MM, are they capable and truly qualified? It would appear that their journey is NOT over, but having only begun. Having a title, and showing that one is worthy of such title are two different ends of a spectrum.

It is the work of each individual in a collective effort that makes a Lodge effective at building its members into our stated purpose of "making good men better". I was taught that Freemasons meet as a Lodge, not in one. Remembering that ritual teaches that ancient lodges met on high hills or low valleys indicates that there wasn't always a fixed location for such meetings as there is now.

Despite the lack of a fixed location, those Masons came prepared to "work" as Masons, and prepared to teach the Craft to younger members, and each other. It would appear that the bonds of brotherly love grew stronger under that system, a system that served well for many years.

I have asked myself what changed. In all my years of reading and study of Freemasonry, it appears to this writer that what changed was one thing we all vowed to never do. Innovation or change can have positive effects on any institution, or individual. It can equally be observed that innovation can have negative impact as well, which in an ideal situation would be spotted quickly and corrected, yet that hasn't always been the case as Masonic and world history has clearly shown those of us who actually read and study.

In this paper I have shared my opinion. I do not expect anyone to agree with me, or my thoughts. I have always strived to keep things as simple as I could so that anyone could grasp some understanding from my words. My final analysis is that we all strive to learn what we can, and be willing to teach it to others.

Freely sharing is something that makes humans distinct, and sharing is what allowed individuals to become unified in common purpose as tribes. We Freemasons are a tribe of sorts, a tribe that becomes family — a family of Brothers.

References:
More Light by H.W. Sanders
An Inconvenient Truth about Freemasonry by Nelson King
Experience of Masonry as a Transformational Art by Robert G. Davis
Anatomy of the Spirit by Caroline Myss, Ph.D.

We are the Working Tools
by Bill Hosler, P.M.

During the three degrees of Freemasonry you are presented with the working tools on the degree in which you are participating. From the gauge to the trowel you are presented with each one and taught their uses, both operative and speculative. These are the tools you are told to use to better yourself and help create your perfect ashlar.

The tools we are given teach everything from how to wisely use our time, rid ourselves of our vices to love your Brother and work with him without ego. If you apply these teachings you will become a better man, citizen, father and husband. But if you have no idea how to apply them these teachings are useless.

These tools are wonderful symbols to help us contemplate the way we live our lives. Our symbolic tools in many ways are like tools an actual workmen would use. Without proper instruction we really can't use them to their fullest potential. The old saying "A workman is only as good as his tools" really holds true. It is much like a man trying to build a house with tools he has never seen before he starts the construction. Proper training ensures you will use these tools in the way in which they were intended to be used and to their fullest potential.

To further illustrate this point if a man wants to use his cordless drill but doesn't charge it before using it the drill won't work. He would be wasting his time and will become frustrated. To make sure his drill will work would be to keep the battery charged at all times. A Mason's tools are much the same way. If a man who takes the time to go through the degrees of Masonry and becomes a Master Mason and then doesn't attend his lodge is much like the uncharged drill. He will slowly lose his passion for the Craft and in the end the teachings of the Fraternity will lose it's power. To be able to fully utilize the tools given him he must charge himself by gathering with his Brethren to socialize and participate in the workings of his lodge and immerse himself in Masonic education. Without charging yourself with the energy of your lodge and it's members your inner battery will grow dim and will soon lose it's charge.

Men are social creatures. Sociologist Charles Cooley called this "The looking glass self" Cooley said "The human mind is social. Beginning as children, humans begin to define themselves within the context of their socialization's."

Each person we encounter throughout our lives helps to mold and shape us into who we are and who we want to be. It starts with your parents and follows you through school into adulthood. Every person we interact with influences our lives and our futures. We have a personal responsibility to use our tools so that when we encounter others, we can be a positive influence in their life.

As we look around our fraternity we encounter other brethren. Many of them, we notice, have the traits and characteristics we wish to emulate. This may be your seated Grand Master, a Past Grand Master, the brother within your lodge or even the old tiler who sits without the door. Each one of them have a lifetime working on themselves and learning through their interactions with other people. Sadly, a Brother who doesn't attend his lodge will lose out of these influences and our teachings will mean nothing to him.

A workman must also maintain and his tools and keep them sharp. If you have a new saw but never use it and instead of putting away properly but instead leaves it outside in the elements the saw will soon become rusty and when you want to use it the saw will be useless.

So it is with your symbolic tools. When the Worshipful Master presents to you these tools and you don't take them to heart and begin to use them after some time they will not be any use to you. Without use they will become dull and rusty and will soon be forgotten. There are many ways in which you can sharpen your skills. Many believe memorizing the ritual is the way this is done.

Memorization is a great way to keep your memory sharp, but without learning the meanings behind the ritual it is equivalent to running a table saw without cutting a piece of wood. The saw blade just spins and nothing is accomplished. By studying the ritual, as well as memorizing it, you will help take the message into your heart thereby protecting it and keeping it sharp.

A nail gun in the hands of a skilled worker is a beautiful thing. It is an essential tool in building, Many great edifices throughout history has been built because of a skilled worker with a hammer. Now nail guns can do the same job faster and with less stress to the body of the worker. It is a wonderful tool but in the hands of a unskilled worker this great tool can be dangerous. Proper knowledge of the use of the tool must be learned before he can use it on a job site. Masonic education is much like the nail gun.

To receive enlightenment from the Craft, education is essential. Today there are many sources where you can seek light. Some sources provide good and wholesome instruction for your labors, but many are less credible. In the past many people have written books, either with good intentions or for mercenary motives which contains inaccurate information. Sadly, many Brethren over the years have gotten information from these spurious sources, taking the information to heart, then communicating it to other Brothers. This is done to the point that this false information has become "Masonic fact" within the Fraternity. Don't fall for these Masonic "Urban legends". Become a student of Freemasonry but please make sure the light you seek is true light.

As each one of us are imperfect ashlars using the working tools provided us to strive for perfection as individuals, we need to gather as friends and brothers to spread the cement of brotherly love as a group. When we attend lodge and interact with other brethren we use each other ashlars to sharpen and hone our symbolic tools. Brethren. We are the working tools.

Finding the Balance
Michael R. Poll, P.M.
Secretary, Louisiana Lodge of Research

Not long ago, a young man turned in his petition to a Masonic lodge. Maybe a relative of his was a Mason or, maybe, he learned of Freemasonry from a popular book or movie. Regardless, he expressed his desire to join. A few weeks after turning in his petition, he received a phone call from a man who told him that he was a member of an investigation committee working on the petition. He asked the young man if he and two other lodge members could come to his house and meet with him. They met at the appointed time. It was a good meeting. Questions were asked and everyone learned a bit more of each other. The committee told the young man that Freemasonry is not an insurance agency. We don't join Masonry with the goal of receiving health benefits or promises of financial assistance. While lodges and Freemasons have a long and honorable history of assisting those in need, Freemasonry is not designed to be a charitable organization, such as the Red Cross. Freemasonry is also not a civic association such as the Jaycees or Lions Club. The primary goal of Freemasonry is to take good men and, through moral instruction, make them better and happier in their lives.

The young man took in all that he was told. He then asked about the history of Freemasonry. He was told that we don't have a complete or clear understanding of all aspects of our beginnings. We know that we are old. As an organization, we go back to 1717 with the creation of the Grand Lodge of England. But, many claim that we can trace ourselves much earlier to the days of the old Operative Freemasons. Many also claim that we can trace our philosophy and manner of symbolic education to an even much earlier time. Sadly, we just don't have definitive answers.

The young petitioner accepted all that he was told and the committee left. Both sides were satisfied. The young man was quietly excited. He knew that what he wanted to join was something very old and very important. He couldn't explain why, but he felt it in his heart. He had done his homework. He had already read the popular books and conducted internet searches of Freemasonry. He knew better than to pay attention to the large amount of flash concerning Freemasonry. He ignored the wild supernatural claims and nonsensical satanic charges. But, he knew that there was something very special about Freemasonry, its manner of instruction by degrees and the whole Masonic philosophy. He felt very good about joining.

In a few weeks, a letter came in the mail telling him that the Lodge had voted on his petition. The ballot was clear and the date of the initiation set. There were many questions that he had forgotten to ask. One thing that he was unsure about was how he should dress for the initiation. He thought about calling, but then remembered some of the books he owned and how the Masons all wore business suits and some even wore tuxedoes. The photos were not all that old, so he thought that he should try to match their dress. He knew that this was something special, but assumed that if they wanted him to wear a tux, they would have told him. So, he decided to wear his suit. When he showed up at the lodge, and to his surprise, many of the members were wearing old blue jeans and equally faded and worn polo shirts — some, t-shirts. Others looked like they were wearing soiled work clothes and had come directly to lodge from work. He felt a bit out of place in such a casual atmosphere. One of the men laughed when he saw him and asked if he was going to church or a wedding.

The young man waited downstairs and was finally called up for the initiation. He felt slightly uncomfortable as the man who came down for him was laughing and told him, "Now, you are in for it!" In for what? What did he mean by that?

He was placed in a little room by a kindly, elderly man who seemed sincerely interested in his well-being. This made him feel better. The degree began.

After the degree was over, the young man had mixed emotions. He knew that what he had experienced was something very important, but why was there so much laughter and talking going on? Why did he hear a considerable amount of yelling out instructions? It was clear that some who spoke did not, at all, know their lines (they were stumbling and fumbling over every few words) and others, from everywhere, were feeding them with what to say (and, loudly). As he was walking around, he also heard about someone's wife being sick and another's cousin who is building a new garage. What did all that have to do with his degree? But, afterwards, everyone was so friendly. Maybe he expected too much. Maybe Freemasonry really is just a group of men who meet to enjoy themselves and try to do antiquated and meaningless ritual every now and then.

In time, the young man's feelings about Masonry changed from those prior to his joining. These were all nice guys. Every time he went to a meeting, he was greeted with smiles, friendly handshakes and inquiries of his health and well-being. There was a mixture of blue collars workers and professional men. All seemed truly interested in the lodge, but they could not really answer even the most basics questions about Freemasonry. It was almost as if Freemasonry and the lodge were two completely different things. Questions concerning the ritual or history were always passed on to one brother who they said was the "answer man." They were a nice group of men — friends — but there was nothing *special* in the lodge; special in the way he viewed Masonry before he joined. This was a club made up of good guys who would meet a couple of times a month to enjoy themselves. They would visit and share a few laughs during a friendly evening. That seemed to be all that he could expect from the lodge experience. The books clearly were speaking of something else. But, what? Who were the Freemasons that he had read about? Did they ever exist? Was it all made up to sell books? After a few months, the young man found that a TV show was scheduled at the same time as his lodge meeting. It was a show that he had wanted to watch for some time. He chose the show over the lodge. Over the next few months and years, it became easier and easier to choose many events over the lodge meetings.

Eventually, the young man attended lodge, maybe, once or twice a year. He made an effort to try to attend some of the important meetings. He did so out of a feeling of obligation, not really enjoyment. He did see some who truly seemed to enjoy each and every meeting. These were the men who kept the lodge alive. At a few meetings, some of the ones who were always there gently scolded him for not attending more of the lodge functions. "You know, the lodge depends on its members and if you don't support the lodge, it will fail." But, what was he to do? Was he obligated to continually go to a place that provided him with no benefit at all other than a few laughs and a meal? He had tried, but after many months of only hearing a reading of the last meeting, bills that needed to be paid, who was sick and discussion of the next planned social event, he grew disinterested. He knew that he could spend his time in more productive ways. So, was he to be blamed as it was suggested? He even read such things from "ranking" Masons who seemed to put all responsibility for the success or failure of a body on his simply attending, regardless of what was offered. The man at the top was never to blame and, even if he was, nothing was ever done. There was no accountability for poor leadership. It was always the rank and file members who seemed to be the responsible parties. The suggestion was that there was some lacking in the young Mason and he needed to wake up and give his total support to whatever was offered. Was there a lacking in him?

Clearly, Freemasonry either failed this young man in about every way possible or there truly was some lacking in him, or a misunderstanding on his part as to the actual nature of Freemasonry. Is Freemasonry only a club made up of good men who try to do charitable work and hold friendly meetings, or is it an organization designed to educate and uplift its members through moral instruction?

On the Grand Lodge of Louisiana website (http://www.la-mason.com), under the tab "Education" and under "What is Freemasonry?" is written: "Freemasonry is the world's oldest and largest fraternity. Its history and tradition date to antiquity. Its singular purpose is to make good men better." OK, that's clear. But, how do we do that? Since this quote was placed under the "Education" tab, maybe that should give us a clue. We should teach and instruct our candidates. The Grand Lodge has a Masonic *Education* Committee. There are countless books and articles written on Masonic education. We learn the importance of education and teaching in our very ritual. But, apart from the ritual, do we actually teach Freemasonry, or is it only words to be spoken or read and not acted upon? How many young men are lost to us simply because we fail to do what we say we will do?

William Lowe Bryan (10th president of Indiana University) wrote: "Education is one of the few things a person is willing to pay for and not get." I believe this is sometimes very true (and has been for a good number of years) regarding Freemasonry. I believe that the hole that was left when quality education ceased to take place in the lodges has been replaced with additional fellowship. That's not a bad thing, but it's not the life blood of Freemasonry. Initiation and making good men "better" is our main reason for existence.

The passing of time is unavoidable. Every year, our lodges hold elections for officers to lead them for the next year. The young men who came into the lodge, but learned very little about Freemasonry, are now in leadership positions. They are the leaders, but truthfully, many are not qualified. To be fair, it's not really their fault. With the speed many of them go through the chairs, how can they help but be inexperienced? They are where they are because someone tapped them on the shoulder and asked them if they would accept a position. They were just trying to be helpful. Maybe the lodge felt that it had no one else to ask and had to take whoever it could get. Maybe it was felt that to take anyone, even someone very inexperienced, was better than closing shop.

Where Masonic education once took place, discussions of lodge picnics or other lodge events now take place. The time that was once spent by the Worshipful Master on the planning of the Masonic education of the members is often now spent on trying to learn the very basics of lodge leadership. Lodge meetings are only as long as felt necessary and then the "enjoyable" time of the lodge takes place — sharing a few laughs with friends. The leaders are expected to keep the members happy, not spend too much money and get through their year with as little hassle as possible. The "hole" was filled and we are marking time, just getting through the years. But, marking time and just getting by does not secure the future of Freemasonry. It is not responsible. It is not enough that we *say* that we are "Freemasonry," but act like a club. We must either be what we say, or admit to being something else.

To all the junior officers of Freemasonry in the state of Louisiana, no matter if you are brand new to Freemasonry, or have been a Mason for a number of years and are only now returning to lodge activity;

no matter what level of experience and knowledge you have — *stop.* Take a breath. You are not alone. You don't have to have a situation where young men are leaving your lodges because of claims that you are not giving them what they expected. You don't have to worry that you will all of a sudden be in charge and not know what in the world to do or say. You have brothers who wish to help you. But, just as each of you had to step up and ask to join Freemasonry, you need to step up and make your needs and desires known. And, when you are a junior officer is the time when you should do this.

The internet is filled with Masonic education websites, but which are reliable? You may wish to seek out the recognized and respected Masonic education sources. Quality Masonic educational societies which you can, and should, join such as The Masonic Society (http://www.themasonicsociety.com); The Philalethes Society (http://www.freemasonry.org), The Masonic Service Association of North America (http://msana.com) and other worthy national organizations are designed to provide quality Masonic educational resources and services. Let's also not forget the excellent Masonic educational material provided by the Louisiana Lodge of Research (http://www.louisianalodgeofresearch.org).

I believe deeply in the importance of finding balance in everything. Going too far one way or the other never seems to bring about what is truly desired. But, what do we do about our present situation? We have already gone too far. Our lodges have taken on more of the appearance of social clubs than lodges of moral instruction. It was not done through maliciousness, it was done out of a desire to help and preserve. It did not happen all at once, but over a period of time. It was done with no ill intentions.

We all know that there is a problem in our lodges. We know that they are not the same lodges as before. We hear the stories of days long gone. Our leaders desire to do good, but some are uncertain as to which path is the best one. None wish for everything to fall apart on their watch. Some may feel that to do nothing is better than to do the wrong thing. Cancer is never cured by inaction.

There is an old Rosicrucian thought that everything felt to be of value must face the test of death. What is truly of value, will come back alive. What is of no value, will fade away. Is Freemasonry of value?

I do not believe that society (or any group of people) are changed in mass by outside stimulus. I believe that change always comes through individual change. When we change as individuals, and if others change in a like manner, then society changes. I believe that the very first step we can take is to recognize that we are in trouble and traveling in the wrong direction. We then need to focus on ourselves and try to make the needed change within *us*. Have you been on an airplane lately? Remember the safety lecture? If you are traveling with someone who may need your assistance in time of emergency, you need to first put on your own oxygen mask so that you will be able to properly help others.

Value is a perception. We place whatever value we choose on something. Value can also change. If you don't treat something as if it is special or valuable, it's not. Anyone who knows me knows that I live in blue jeans. But, those who only know me from lodge believe that I live in suits. Going to lodge is something very, very special to me. I dress accordingly. If I did not own a suit, I would clean myself and wear the best shirt and slacks I owned.

Everyone, try this the next time you visit your lodge: act as if it is a *very* special occasion; as if you are going to a *very* special place to do *very* special things. Do what you would do if you were going to such a special event. Fix your mind to always treat going to lodge as something *very* important and special. Make that one permanent change in your life. After you have done this, join or take advantage of what is offered in one of the above Masonic education services or societies. Freemasonry will be what its members make it. The true and sole power within Freemasonry is where it has always been, with its members — with you.

Cathleen Whigham
New Orleans, Lady of the Valley
Louis J. Caruso, P.G.M.
The Grand Lodge of Louisiana

Reproduced from the November-December, 2005 edition of The Scottish Rite Journal

Cathleen Whigham will complete 60 years of faithful service in 2006 with the New Orleans Scottish Rite Valley.

January 19, 1946, appeared to be a routine day at the Scottish Rite in New Orleans. According to the local newspaper, it was cloudy and rain was imminent. However, the routine would soon change for Ill. Edward Cunny, 33°, then the Valley Secretary. As he was tending to his duties, in through the door walked a bright energetic young lady who was smiling from ear to ear. Ill. Cunny asked, "What can I do for you young lady?" She said her name was Cathleen Whigham, "with a C and not a K," and added that she had come to bring some joy and happiness to his life. He responded with a chuckle and wanted to know just how she was hoping to do that. Cathleen informed him she was looking for employment, and that if he hired her he would never regret doing so. Bro. Cunny laughed and said, "Young lady, I like your mettle. You have my vote, but I have to present it to the Hiring Committee."

Miss Whigham soon appeared before the Hiring Committee, composed of 13 members of the Consistory, and immediately won them over with her bright smile and sunny disposition. It wouldn't be appropriate to give her age at that time, but let's just say that with today's regulations, the good brothers would probably have received a summons for violating the country's Child Labor Laws!

During her 59-year and 10-month tenure with the New Orleans Scottish Rite, Miss Cathleen Whigham has trained a total of seven Scottish Rite Secretaries in the performance of their duties. Each and every one of them has prospered under her guidance and has performed in an outstanding manner to her satisfaction. She was with us before the advent of the electric typewriter, the fax machine, and the computer, but she has made good use of those as they became available. Miss Whigham possesses a wealth of knowledge about the Scottish Rite and is always prepared to consult with anyone looking for such information. She is a walking encyclopedia of the New Orleans Scottish Rite Valley.

Miss Whigham personally knows or remembers each and every one of the members of our Valley (past and present), and at one time or another has assisted them in their travels through life. It is not surprising that anyone who has passed through the doors of the New Orleans Scottish Rite Consistory has never forgotten Cathleen Whigham. She is there each and every day, rain or shine, hot or cold. Every person who has visited the New Orleans Valley fondly remembers meeting Miss Whigham.

The New Orleans Scottish Rite Valley, located at 619 Carondelet St., New Orleans, Louisiana, is the oldest Valley in continuous existence today. The building was constructed in 1850, and has been placed on the National Register of Historic Places. It was purchased by the Grand Consistory of Louisiana on May 1, 1905, and has been our domicile since then.

We hope that Miss Cathleen Whigham will be with us for many more years and will continue to bring her special kind of sunshine into our lives. We were fortunate when she decided to seek employment with the New Orleans Scottish Rite, for she has indeed brought joy and happiness to our lives, as well as dedication and devotion to her job. She is definitely the "Lady of our Valley."

Epilogue

This article was written in the summer of 2005 in anticipation of Miss Whigham's 60th anniversary with the New Orleans Scottish Rite.

Little could we foresee the devastation of hurricane Katrina. Miss Whigham is a hardy soul and had decided to weather the hurricane in her apartment. However, high winds blew the roof off and the waters started rising. This was too much for even a seasoned New Orleans resident, so she waded out to her car and drove out of the city before the levee broke and the flood waters came in. She drove west for five days until she arrived at Tucson to stay with her brother. She is well, but understandably upset because she lost everything. The brothers in New Orleans are also upset that their "Lady of the Valley" is not with them. They have promised to find Miss Whigham another apartment and look forward to her homecoming, which will signal the start of a return to normalcy.

Editor's Note: In the epilogue, the events of Hurricane Katrina are explained during which Miss Whigham relocated to her brother's home in Tucson, Arizona. The hopes for her to return to New Orleans were not realized and Miss Whigham remained in Tucson until the time of her passing, October 26, 2014.

Meeting on the Level
by J. Quincy Gotte

As Masons, we are to be reminded of the "long and arduous, but necessary, struggle for a people to pass from slavery to freedom, from degradation and ignorance to civilization and enlightenment, from spiritual bondage to spiritual liberty." We should also be reminded that "the life of virtue is not a life of ease but of constant struggle." Rex R. Hutchens –"A Bridge to Light"

As Masons, we are to encourage liberty, equality and commitment within the hearts of all people while maintaining dignity and honor. (Rex R. Hutchens – "A bridge to Light")

The Degrees in Masonry teach us to persevere and remain encouraged through difficult times. If the tasks we are obligated to in Masonry were easy, perseverance and a sense of honor and dignity would not be needed. As with all great tasks, costs should be analyzed, desires should be circumscribed and commitments should be reaffirmed.

"The first lesson which one learns, who engages in any great work of reform or beneficence, is that men are essentially careless, lukewarm, and indifferent as to everything that does not concern their own personal and immediate welfare." (Albert Pike –"Morals & Dogma")

I believe that equality is the basis of all freedom, and that our work is faced with the challenging reality of polarity. With every desire to do a good work toward humanity, there are other forces at work that are positioned against it and stand a risk in losing something it has achieved or is trying to achieve. I believe that the Grand Architect, Blessed be He, has created all things, and that nothing was created in vain. I believe He uses His creation to bring about miracles, corrections and rewards in ways that may be seen as extraordinary, and at other times seen as ordinary. With that said, there is a psychological element within a spiritual and physical event. Whenever an individual, religion or nation sees itself as superior to others or inferior to others, an atmosphere of inequality is generated.

This type of atmosphere causes a lack of trust, honor and duty, and makes it nearly impossible to bring about without devastating adjustments, the good that was originally intended. There will always be opposition that will not want the greater good and would prefer a selfish gain; also, there will be feuding sides that want the same thing, but lack the necessary elements needed to bring about success. A good Ambassador is able to communicate the goals and positions of their party in a way that will create a trusting and honorable atmosphere with the other party involved, and generate an obligation of duty towards each other. They would be able to recognize and appreciate every interested position and applicable ability, and would be able to communicate the value in them. The first step in the process of communication is known to every Mason as meeting on the level. If this first step is not taken, all other steps will stumble within the compromise.

All events, past, present, and future, were foreseen and approved by a higher power with the intent of the greater good, and the greater good will ultimately take place. Every soul has the chance to partake in the bestowal of blessings upon humanity. It is completely understandable that organizations, religions, corporations, and nations are used by our Creator in bringing about this bestowal of blessings that our existence needs and enjoys. Sometimes, the individual may feel dwarfed compared to the massive achievements of the aforementioned, and undervalue their unique ability within this process. This feeling could lead to the old saying "I gave at the office" or "that's what I pay taxes for". After this position is accepted within our hearts and minds, we may start to think that how we treat others immediately around us isn't as important as making that donation, and we then conform ourselves to the ordinary. To lower the bar to whatever our daily congregation accepts to be as normal and usual behavior, is to lose our identity and individuality. To treat another soul as if they are below us to the point that we cannot reach them, or above us to the point that we despise them, will cripple the process of our individuality in the bestowal of blessings. As Masons, we need to realize daily that we are the face of our great Brotherhood; and the mindset and behavior that is displayed to the individuals we interact with each day speaks loudly about Freemasonry. I can't think of a more honorable or successful life than the virtuous life of a soul that has fervently sought out and performed the greater good towards the individuals within that soul's ability.

"Masonry teaches, that of all the events and actions, that take place in the universe of worlds and the eternal succession of ages, there is not one,… which God did not forever foresee, with all the distinctness of immediate vision, combining all, so that man's free will should be His instrument, like the other forces of nature. It teaches that the soul of man is formed by Him for the purpose; that, built up in its proportions and fashioned in every part, by infinite skill, an emanation from His spirit, its nature, necessity, and design are virtue. It is so formed,… so exquisitely proportioned in every part, that sin introduced into it is misery… it is made for virtue not vice." (Albert Pike – "Morals & Dogma")

As Masons, we must recognize our equality with each other and all others, and always meet on the level.

Books referenced: Albert Pike – "Morals & Dogma"
Rex R. Hutchens – "A Bridge to Light"

Forgiveness and Freemasonry
by Michael R. Poll, P.M.

The act of forgiving is a cornerstone tenet of most religions. Christianity is built around the concept of the Grand Architect forgiving the sins of the deserving. Likewise, Freemasonry teaches the concept of seeking forgiveness in its most basic teachings. In the closing prayer of lodges forgiveness is sought from the Almighty: "Pardon, we beseech Thee, whatever Thou hast seen amiss in us ..." (Louisiana Masonic Monitor p.15). We are taught that humans are far from perfect creatures, and if we could not seek redemption for our transgressions, then our lives could be seen as hopeless.

We are also taught that forgiveness is not only something that should be *sought*, but that we should *extend* forgiveness to those who have wronged us. "And when you stand praying, if you hold anything against anyone, forgive him, so that your Father in heaven may forgive you your sins." (Mark 11:25)

The extending of forgiveness to another human is sometimes, however, a point of confusion. Why are we forgiving this person? What is the benefit of forgiving another? What conditions must exist before we can extend forgiveness? What is expected after we forgive someone?

If we can not clearly understand why we are forgiving someone, or what it means to forgive, then it would seem to be a pointless and empty act. One concept is that when we forgive someone, the one being forgiven is the one who benefits. This belief, however, does not provide satisfactory answers to all questions. What if the one being forgiven does not seek or care about forgiveness? In addition, the sometimes spoken, and sometimes implied, condition for forgiveness is that the offense is not repeated. Do repeated offenses or refusal to request forgiveness give cause for it to be withheld?

In Freemasonry, we are taught that the Bible is to be the rule and guide to our faith and practices. If this is so, then the Bible does not always seem to require that forgiveness be sought by our fellow man. In Matthew 18:21-22, the Bible simply tells us to forgive others (and to do so as often as needed). "Then Peter came to Jesus and asked, 'Lord, how many times shall I forgive my brother when he sins against me? Up to seven times?' Jesus answered, 'I tell you, not seven times, but seventy-seven times.' "

If forgiving the one who causes the offence is to be extended even if it is not requested/wanted and even if the same offense occurs again and again, then does this mean that the Bible is telling us to be rather foolish? Does it mean that there are no consequences for our actions and one should be rewarded for bad behavior? I do not believe so.

The perceived problem may come from our associating and linking forgiveness with consequences. Forgiveness is relational. Consequences are circumstantial. If during an angry argument, we were to take the treasured, antique vase of a loved one and throw it to the ground breaking it into tiny pieces, what happens next? Well, that depends on the parties involved. If we sincerely apologized for our actions, it is very possible that our loved one will forgive us and we can move on from the event. But, nothing we can ever do will erase the fact that the vase was destroyed. That's done and is a consequence of our actions. It can't be undone.

In the Bible, Paul wrote, "Do not be deceived: God cannot be mocked. People reap what they sow." (Gal. 6:7). Forgiveness for our actions does not mean that there are no consequences for those actions.

Let's take Freemasonry and try to apply this thought. Let's say that your lodge has a family night where Masons and non-Masons are enjoying a very nice dinner in your lodge hall. A well-liked member of the lodge comes into the hall obviously drunk. He soon begins to cause disturbances. Someone mentions his condition to him and this only outrages him. He begins throwing over tables and creates a major disturbance. This alone is grounds for a Masonic trial. Masons do not act this way. But Masons are also taught to help each other and lift up a fallen brother. Let's say that a few days after the event, the member contacts the lodge officers and gives a heartfelt apology for what happened. He explains of some unfortunate personal events in his life that caused him to break in such a manner. The officers can not point to any like event by this brother in the past and believe that he is truly sorry for his actions. They deliberate. After some thought and consideration of the events, Masonic charity comes into play. They do not file Masonic charges on him and only advise him to take better control of his life.

Did the lodge officers act improperly by not insisting that he face trial? I don't believe so. They fully realized that this was a very serious situation. They weighed all aspects of what happened and what they should do. This was not something that the brother had done before, it was unlike him, he expressed sincere regret, and gave assurance that it would not happen again. As humans, we all fail from time to time. I believe that nothing more could be done and that they acted responsibly for the good of the Order. They forgave him.

Now, let's go forward a bit in time. It's now the end of the year and the brother who caused the disturbance has not again shown up at lodge drunk and has caused no further disturbances. The lodge has a large family event for presenting awards to various members. The brother who caused the drunken disturbance is named "Mason of the Year" and given a beautiful plaque and called up before the lodge for pictures with the Worshipful Master. What is the message being given?

When we deal with consequences there is no right or wrong, no moral or immoral, there is only cause and effect. What we might want or desire does not offset the consequence resulting from an event.

Whatever the intention of the Worshipful Master in giving this brother this award (even if he feels it is a noble reason), this selection could objectively be seen as inappropriate based on what happened earlier in the year. The reasonable result is to portray Freemasonry as a group that rewards (or, does not care about) bad behavior. This is the message sent and received no matter what the Worshipful Master or lodge desired or intended. It is the consequence of selecting this particular member for this award. And, with it, the reputation of Freemasonry may be permanently damaged for all who remember the drunken display.

The lodge officers honored their obligation to who they believed to be a deserving brother, but they were also obligated to protect the reputation of our Order. They should have looked more objectively at the entire picture and selected another deserving brother for this award. Both the drunken member and the lodge officers failed in different ways, and both actions resulted in consequences. Good judgment was not used in either case.

And what of the predicament when we are told that we must forgive, but the offender does not seek forgiveness or continues with his objectionable behavior? Unconditional forgiveness can be seen as an affront against justice and a denial of the significance of the wrongdoing and its damaging effects. The Bible even presents us with what could be viewed as a contradictory message from the ones given earlier: "If your brother or sister sins against you, rebuke them; and if they repent, forgive them. Even if they sin against you seven times in a day and seven times come back to you saying 'I repent,' you must forgive them." (Luke 17:3-4) Notice how the act of forgiveness is qualified ("if they repent"). If they don't repent, then the suggestion here is that they should not be forgiven.

This goes to the questions of *why* we should forgive and what *is* forgiveness? Forgiveness can be seen as a pardon for offenses or a release of negative feelings, depending on how the act of forgiveness is used. In both cases, forgiveness is a choice. The consequence is not a choice, but the result of an action. If someone accidently bumps into you in a store, the polite thing for them to do is apologize. The event is usually soon forgotten and the consequences of the act are so minor that they are also soon forgotten. If one is rude enough to bump into you and walk away with no apology or even arrogance over the event, the memory of the event may remain longer, but since it is still minor, it will pass away before very long. Serious acts, however, may never be forgotten and can change (or completely destroy) the nature of even close relationships.

In truth, we should not forgive for the benefit of others, but for our own benefit. It is understood that sometimes a person does not intend on changing his behavior. He may not care about what anyone thinks of his actions. We don't forgive him for his sake, but because having anger, hurt and upset within us does not help us in any manner. Negative feelings tear us down and prevent us from doing the good that we should be doing. We are not pardoning an act, but letting it go so that it does not drag us down. We have no ability to change another, but we have total control over what we think and how we act. We *can* change our outlook. We *can* choose to let go of feelings that can lead to bitterness. It does not mean that there are no consequences for actions. There may be no pardon for the act and relationships may be forever destroyed because of it, but you do not have to carry anger within you. This *is* a form of forgiveness. It means only that we wish to live in peace and choose to let go of pain.

In Masonry we are taught that if we have a serious issue with another Mason, then we should try to work out the problem. If we can not, we should not risk the peace and harmony of the lodge and we should withdraw from a meeting rather than allow the lodge to suffer. There is a message here. We *can* forgive someone, have peace in our heart, but because of past actions, not have a close relationship (or, any at all) with someone who has wronged us. We can walk away from the "meeting" for the sake of peace and harmony. We are in control of our own feelings and actions.

UNITED GRAND LODGES OF GERMANY (VGLv D)
by Clayton J. Borne III, P.G.M.
Worshipful Master, Louisiana Lodge of Research

Following my meeting with the German Grand Master, M.W. Bro. Klause Kopp, at the 10th World Conference of Grand Masters, he tendered through his Grand Secretary information on the structure of the fraternity in Germany. I found the present structure of the VGLvD (Acronym for Vereinigte Grosslogen von Deutschiand), to be most interesting.

Historically German Freemasonry can trace its origins back to September 13, 1740, when the "Grosse National Mutterloge zu den drei Weltkugeln" (Translation: Grand National Mother Lodge of the Three World Globes) was established as the first Grand Lodge in Germany, by Frederick the Great, who served as its first Grand Master. This Lodge still proudly exists today as part of the VGLvD.

The VGLvD can best be described as a <u>FEDERATION</u> of five Grand Lodges, united to form one <u>SOVEREIGN</u> Grand Body for Germany. This unification originally was designed to accomplish two basic goals; First, to facilitate the need to regain recognition for German Freemasonry after the debacle of World Was II; Second, to unite different Masonic 'systems' existing within the remnants of Freemasonry in Germany. The VGLvD was formed, and the constituting Grand Lodges united under the terms of what is called the "Magna Charta" (Pronounced Karta) of German Freemasonry. The Magna Charta, the 'constitution' of the VGLvD, can perhaps be more appropriately termed 'Articles of Confederation'. The Magna Charta has been amended several times, and under its authority, laws and regulations for the government of the VGLvD have been adopted. Following is a listing of the five constituent of 'partner' Grand Lodges which comprise the VGLvD, shown in the order in which they became signatures to the Magna Charta of Freemasonry in Germany:

1. <u>Grossloge A.F.u.A.M. von Deutschland</u>: Sometimes referred to simply as "AFAM". This Grand Lodge was established through consolidation of surviving members of seven pre-World War II Grand Lodges.

2. <u>Grosse Landesloge der Freimaurer van Deutschland</u>: Sometimes referred to as "FvD" (Referring to <u>F</u>reimaurer <u>O</u>rden"). The FvD is part of a complete 'system' of Masonic degrees based on the so-called Swedish of Scandinavian Rite. Christian dogma is highly stressed within the FvD system, especially in its advanced degrees, which in some ways can be equated with the American York Rite system.

3. <u>Grosse National-Mutterloge "Zu den drei Weltkugelllln"</u>: The oldest Grand Lodge in Germany, it is often referred to simply as "3WK" (Three World Globes). Time and the partition of Germany (We must remember its greatest strength was in Prussis!) have taken its toll. This Grand Lodge's system also includes additional steps or degrees known as "Erkenntnisstufen".

4. <u>Grand Lodge of British Freemasons in Germany</u>: Often very simply referred to as "the Brits", "BFG", this Grand Lodge is composed predominantly of British Forces personnel, with the result that more than half the total membership is not physically resident in Germany.

5. <u>American-Canadian Grand Lodge, A.F.&A.M.</u>: Generally referred to simply as "ACGL", this jurisdiction is composed predominantly of members of the American and Canadian Forces or government personnel stationed in Germany, subject to constant turnover resulting from reassignments; most of its current membership is not physically resident in Germany.

In almost every other jurisdiction, reference to the Grand Lodge is always simply "The Grand Lodge". In Germany, almost always the Brothers use the acronym or nickname – even for the VGLvD itself. This may be a natural result of the proliferation of Bodies, or simply the result of the German penchant for abbreviating everything.

The MAGNA CHARTA clearly states the constituent Grand Lodges are <u>autonomous</u>; they govern their own internal affairs. The Magna Charta also contains rules for electing a Grand Master and one Deputy Grand Master; regulations for the regular convening of a Communication (called "Konvent" in German: a word akin to the English convention); and various other rules for the government of the VGLvD. There are no Grand Wardens in the VGLvD; but a grand Treasurer and a Grand Secretary are part of the so-called "Grossmeisteramt" (Grand Master's Bureau). The governing organ of the VGL is the 'Senate', composed of members elected or appointed by their respective Grand Lodges, based on a proportionate membership representation, and in the interest of continuity most are mortally reelected or appointed for successive terms. Several committees exist, which are appointed or confirmed by the Senate.

Since the VGLvD is recognized and acknowledged as the Sovereign Grand Lodge in Germany, each constituent Grand Lodge enjoys recognition as the result of its membership in the VGLvD. Fraternal relations with the other Grand Lodges, including any exchange of representatives, are strictly within the sphere of responsibility of the VGLvD. Generally, correspondence between Grand Lodges must be channeled through the VGLvD, except when this authority is delegated. A prime example of this delegation may be noted in the fact the ACGL has conducted all of its vast correspondence direct to all other jurisdictions, as the VGLvD is neither administratively nor financially in a position to handle the administrative requirements of the ACGL.

While the five partner Grand Lodges are autonomous and govern their internal affairs without interference, specific restrictions are placed on their activities. As 'subordinate' Grand Lodges, those matters normally construed as the inherent right or responsibility of a Sovereign Grand Lodge (In the sense of absolute responsibility and authority for a territorial jurisdiction, they cannot individually preempt the prerogatives or rights of the VGLvD. As the VGLvD is the guarantor of recognition with all other Grand Lodes, it bears the ultimate responsibility of ensuring that all lodges working under its sovereign authority are regular.

In effect, a 'federal' or 'collective' voice exists for recognized Freemasonry in Germany, and as the result of this 'partnership' in the VGLvD, each partner is involved in the decision-making process in regard to those matters and laws affecting all Freemasons in Germany.

Needless to say, as in any federal system, efforts to effect better coordination among the partner Grand Lodges, as well as efforts to establish greater uniformity in respect of certain Masonic procedures are among the many subjects that constantly involve the Grand Master and the Senate. On-going attempts to define and regulate these and other important Masonic matters are undertaken at the regularly scheduled meetings of the Senate and the several Senate committees.

The KONVENT is the regularly convened Communication of the United Grand Lodges of Germany. As currently regulated, the Konvent is convened every three years for the purpose of electing a new Grand Master and Deputy Grand Master, who serve for a three-year period. Each Lodge is entitled to one vote at the Konvent, and that vote can only be exercised by the Master, one of the Wardens in succession, or by a proxy as specified in the regulations governing the Konvent.

Interim Convents may be called at any time, but these would be more ceremonial in nature, with legislation normally not introduced except in emergency circumstances. The Grand Master of the VGLvD, together with the Senate, determines when and where Convents may be called in the intervening years. The triennial Konvent is normally held in the City of Berlin, the official domicile or seat of the VGLvd. The Grand Masters successor for the next three years is elected and installed.

It is hoped this article will be of some assistance in helping the Brethren to better understand the complexities of the organization of the Masonic fraternity in Germany. It is a structure that is unique in the world of Freemasonry; however one that has proved exceedingly workable. It stands as a living monument to the ability of Masons to harmoniously exemplify vital Masonic ideals.

The North Star
by J. Quincy Gotte

The center most point of your interest...

Throughout history, we have seen the rise and fall of empires and religions, and both its wondrous advances and devastations towards society. They have at times condemned and put to death men and women whom it considered, at that time, to be heretics or enemies of the state; as history unfolds, time may reveal a clearer picture, the lives that were taken from those condemned men and women may become recognized and honored as martyrs for truth, hope, and justice by that same government or religion. Some have turned the gods of one religion into the angels and demons of another. History itself, in times, may have fallen victim and taken as one of the spoils of war. You may have experienced betrayal by a friend, a partner, a family member, or a loved one whom you trusted and held in high regard. Indeed, the winds of change have always blown throughout history and will continue to do so in our lives and beyond. We all walk in partial light, and our lamps illuminate only so far beyond our steps. But still, we must move forward regardless of the uncertainty that looms in the darkness ahead. There is no certainty of what tomorrow holds for any of us. It may be that the next sunrise favors you and puts you in a fortunate position to be a blessing to another, or perhaps you will be put in a less fortunate position and be in need of your brother's blessing.

"We seem never to know what any thing means or is worth until we have lost it. We never know the full significance of the words, 'property,' 'ease,' and 'health'; the wealth of meaning in the fond epithets, 'parent,' child,' beloved,' and 'friend,' until the thing or the person is taken away; until, in place of the bright, visible being, comes the awful and desolate shadow, where nothing is: where we stretch out our hands in vain, and strain our eyes upon dark and dismal vacuity. Yet, in that vacuity, we do not lose the object that we loved. It becomes only the more real to us. Our blessings not only brighten when they depart, but are fixed in enduring reality; and love and friendship receive their everlasting seal under the cold impress of death." –Albert Pike-"Morals & Dogma"

During all of the storms and calms of life, wisdom has always and will continue to cry out and find rest in the bosom of that soul who hungers after her and hears her voice, thirsting after righteousness, and seeking knowledge. Indeed that soul will find a balance, equally dispensed from both light and dark times. That soul will understand the harmony of the two, and will be able to bridle its chaotic toil.

"There are greater and better things in us all, than the world takes account of, or than we take note of; if we would but find them out." – Albert Pike-"Morals & Dogma"

All of this wisdom, righteousness, and knowledge would not be desired or obtained without the graces of our Creator and His Will, Blessed be He. A heavenly interest is in the creation, and is active and divinely invested throughout each day. God, Blessed be He, has always provided an open line of communication with His creation, and takes pleasure in that communion; this is where these jewels of life are given. Because the creation is constantly being created; a daily communion, belief, and faith in The Creator, is crucial to the center most point of our interest.

"It is the soul alone that gives any value to the things of this world; and it is only by raising the soul to its just elevation above all other things, that we can look rightly upon the purposes of this earth."-Albert Pike-"Morals & Dogma"

The Powers of the Worshipful Master

Carl Claudy, P.G.M.
The Short Talk Bulletin Aug. 1929

The incumbent of the Oriental Chair has powers peculiar to his station; powers far greater than those of the President of a society or the Chairman of a meeting of any kind. President and Chairman are elected by the body over which they preside, and may be removed by that body. A Master is elected by his lodge, but he cannot be removed by it; only by the grand Master or Grand Lodge. The presiding officer is bound by rules of order adopted by the body and by its by-laws. A lodge cannot pass by-laws to alter, amend or curtail the powers of a Master. Its by-laws are subject to approval by the proper Grand Lodge Committee or by the Grand Master; seldom are any approved which infringe upon his ancient prerogatives and powers; in those few instances in which improper by-laws have been approved, subsequent rulings have often declared the Master right in disregarding them.

Grand Lodges differ in their interpretation of some of the "ancient usages and customs" of the Fraternity; what applies in one Jurisdiction does not necessarily apply in another. But certain powers of a Master are so well recognized that they may be considered universal. The occasional exceptions, if any, but prove the rule. The Master may congregate his lodge when he pleases, and for what purpose he wishes, "provided" it does not interfere with the laws of the Grand Lodge. For instance, he may assemble his lodge as a Special Communication to confer degrees, at his pleasure; but he must not, in so doing, contravene that requirement of the grand Lodge which calls for proper notice to the brethren, nor may a Master confer a degree in less than the statutory time following a preceding degree without a dispensation from the Grand Master.

The Master has the right of presiding over and controlling his lodge, and only the Grand Master, or his Deputy, may suspend him. He may put any brother in the East to preside or to confer a degree; he may then resume the gavel at his pleasure - even in the middle of a sentence if he wants to! But even when he has delegated authority temporarily, the Master is not relieved from responsibility for what occurs in his lodge.

It is the Master's right to control lodge business and work. It is in a very real sense "his" lodge. He decides all points of order and no appeal from his decision may be taken to the lodge. He can initiate and terminate debate at his pleasure, he can second any motion, propose any motion, vote twice in the case of a tie (not universal), open and close at his pleasure, with the usual exception that he may not open a Special Communication at an hour earlier than that given in the notice, or a Stated Communication earlier than the hour stated in the by-laws, without dispensation from the Grand Master. He is responsible only to the Grand Master and the Grand Lodge, the obligations he assumed when he was installed, his conscience and his God.

The Master has the undoubted right to say who shall enter, and who must leave the lodge room. He may deny any visitor entrance; indeed, he may deny a member the right to enter his own lodge, but he must have a good and sufficient reason therefore, otherwise his Grand Lodge will unquestionably rule such a drastic step arbitrary and punish accordingly. "Per contra," if he permits entry of a visitor to whom some member has objected, he may also subject himself to Grand Lodge discipline. In other words, his "power" to admit or exclude is absolute; his "right" to admit or exclude is hedged about by pledges he takes at his installation and the rules of the Grand Lodge.

A very important power of the Master is that of appointing committees. No lodge may appoint a committee. The lodge may pass a resolution that a committee be appointed, but the selection of that committee is an inherent right of the Master. He is, "ex officio," a member of all committees he appoints. The reason is obvious; he is responsible for the conduct of his lodge to the Grand Master and the Grand Lodge. If the lodge could appoint committees and act upon their recommendations, the Master would be in the anomalous position of having great responsibilities, and no power to carry out their performance.

The Master, and only the Master, may order a committee to examine a visiting brother. It is his responsibility to see that no cowan or eavesdropper comes within the tiled door. Therefore, it is for him to pick a committee in which he has confidence. So, also, with the committees which report upon petitioners. He is responsible for the accuracy, fair-mindedness, the speed and intelligence of such investigations. It is, therefore, for him to say to whom shall be delegated this necessary and important duty.

It is generally, not exclusively, held that only the Master can issue a summons. The dispute, where it exists, is over the right of members present at a Stated Communication to summons the whole membership.

It may now be interesting to look for a moment at some matters in which the Worshipful Master is not supreme, and catalog a few things he may "not" do.

The Master, and only the Master appoints the appointive officers in his lodge. In most Jurisdictions he may remove such appointed officers at his pleasure. But, he cannot suspend, or deprive of his station or place, any officer elected by the lodge. The Grand Master or his Deputy, may do this; the Worshipful Master may not.

A Master may not spend lodge money without the consent of the lodge. As a matter of convenience, a Master frequently does pay out money in sudden emergencies, looking to the lodge for reimbursement. But he cannot spend any lodge funds without the permission of the lodge. Some Jurisdictions do allow the lodge by-laws to permit the Master to spend emergency funds up to a specified amount without prior consent of the lodge.

A Master cannot accept a petition, or confer a degree without the consent of the lodge. It is for the lodge, not the Master, to say from what men it will receive an application, or a petition; and upon what candidates degrees shall be conferred. The Master has the same power to "reject" through the "black cube" as any member has, but no power whatever to "accept" any candidate against the will of the lodge.

The lodge, not the Master, must approve or disapprove the minutes of the preceding meeting. The Master cannot approve them; had he that power he might, with the connivance of the secretary, "run wild" in his lodge, and still his minutes would show no trace of his improper conduct. But the Master may refuse to put a motion to confirm or approve minutes which he believes to be inaccurate or incomplete; in this way he can prevent a careless, headstrong Secretary from doing what he wants with his minutes! Should a Master refuse to permit minutes to be confirmed, the matter would naturally be brought before the Grand Lodge or the Grand Master for settlement.

A Master cannot suspend the by-laws. He must not permit the lodge to suspend the by-laws. If the lodge wishes to change them, the means are available, not in suspension; but, in amendment. An odd exception may be noted, which has occurred in at least one Grand Jurisdiction, and doubtless may occur in others. A very old lodge adopted by-laws shortly after it was constituted, which by-laws were approved by a young Grand Lodge before that body had, apparently, devoted much attention to these important rules.

For many years this lodge carried in its by-laws and "order of business" which specified, among other things, that following the reading of the minutes, the next business was balloting. As the time of meeting of this lodge was early (seven o'clock) this by-law worked a hardship for years, compelling brethren who wished to vote to hurry to lodge, often at great inconvenience.

At last a Master was elected who saw that the by-law interfered with his right to conduct the business of the lodge as he thought proper. He balloted at what he thought was the proper time, the last order of business, not the first. An indignant committee of Past Masters, who preferred the old order, applied to the Grand Master for relief. The Grand Master promptly ruled that "order of business" in the by-laws could be no more than suggestive, not mandatory; and that the Worshipful Master had the power to order a ballot on a petition at the hour which seemed to him wise, provided - and this was stressed - that he ruled wisely, and did not postpone a ballot until after a degree, or until so late in the evening that brethren wishing to vote upon it had left the lodge room.

A Worshipful Master has no more right to invade the privacy which shrouds the use of the "Black Cube" (or Ball), or which conceals the reason for an objection to an elected candidate receiving the degrees, than the humblest member of the lodge. He cannot demand disclosure of action or motive from any brother, and should he do so, he would be subject to the severest discipline from the Grand Lodge.

Grand Lodges usually argue that a dereliction of duty by a brother who possesses the ability and character to attain the East, is worse than that of some less informed brother. The Worshipful Master receives great honor, has great privileges, enjoys great prerogatives and powers. Therefore, he must measure up to great responsibilities. A Worshipful Master cannot resign. Vacancies occur in the East through death, suspension by a Grand Master, expulsion from the Fraternity. No power can make a Master attend to his duties if he desires to neglect them. If he will not, or does not attend to them, the Senior Warden presides. He is, however, still Senior Warden; he does not become Master until elected and installed.

In broad outline, these are the important and principal powers and responsibilities of a Worshipful Master, considered entirely from the standpoint of the "ancient usages and customs of the Craft." Nothing is said here of the moral and spiritual duties which devolve upon a Master.

Volumes might be and some have been written upon how a Worshipful Master should preside, in what ways he can "give the brethren good and wholesome instruction," and upon his undoubted moral responsibility to do his best to leave his lodge better than he found it. Here we are concerned only with the legal aspect of his powers and duties.

Briefly then, if he keeps within the laws, resolutions and edicts of his Grand Lodge on the one hand, and the Landmarks, Old Charges, Constitutions and "ancient usages and customs" on the other, the power of the Worshipful Master is that of an absolute monarch. His responsibilities and his duties are those of an apostle of Light!

He is a gifted brother who can fully measure up to the use of his power and the power of his leadership.

The Old Charges of Freemasonry
By H. L. Haywood
The Builder, September 1923

WHAT THE OLD CHARGES ARE

I have just come from reading an article in one of the more obscure masonic periodicals in which an unknown brother lets go with this very familiar remark: "As for me, I am not interested in the musty old documents of the past. I want to know what is going on today." The context makes it clear that he had in mind the Old Charges. A sufficient reply to this ignoramus is that the Old Charges are among the things that are "going on today." Eliminate them from Freemasonry as it now functions and not a subordinate lodge, or a Grand Lodge, or any other regular masonic body could operate at all; they are to what the Constitution of this nation is to the United States government, and what its statutes are to every state in the Union. All our constitutions, statutes, laws, rules, by-laws and regulations to some extent or other hark back to the Old Charges, and without them masonic jurisprudence, or the methods for governing and regulating the legal affairs of the Craft, would be left hanging suspended in the air. In proportion as masonic leaders, Grand Masters, Worshipful Masters and Jurisprudence Committees ignore, or forget, or misunderstand these masonic charters they run amuck, and lead the Craft into all manner of wild and unmasonic undertakings. If some magician could devise a method whereby a clear conception of the Old Charges and what they stand for could be installed into the head of every active mason in the land, it would save us all from embarrassment times without number and it would relieve Grand Lodges and other Grand bodies from the needless expenditure of hundreds of thousands of dollars every year. If there is any practical necessity, any hard down-next-to-the-ground necessity anywhere in Freemasonry today, it is for a general clear-headed understanding of the Ancient Constitutions and landmarks of our Order.

By the OLD CHARGES is meant those ancient documents that have come down to us from the fourteenth century and afterwards in which are incorporated the traditional history, the legends and the rules and regulations of Freemasonry. They are called variously

"Ancient Manuscripts", "Ancient Constitutions", "Legend of the Craft", "Gothic Manuscripts", "Old Records", etc, etc. In their physical makeup these documents are sometimes found in the form of handwritten paper or parchment rolls, the units of which are either sewn or pasted together; of hand-written sheets stitched together in book form, and in the familiar printed form of a modern book. Sometimes they are found incorporated in the minute book of a lodge. They range in estimated date from 1390 until the first quarter of the eighteenth century, and a few of them are specimens of beautiful Gothic script. The largest number of them are in the keeping of the British Museum; the masonic library of West Yorkshire, England, has in custody the second largest number.

As already said these Old Charges (such is their most familiar appellation) form the basis of modern masonic constitutions, and therefore jurisprudence. They establish the continuity of the masonic institution through a period of more than five centuries, and by fair implication much longer; and at the same time, and by token of the same significance, prove the great antiquity of Masonry by written documents, which is a thing no other craft in existence is able to do. These manuscripts are traditional and legendary in form and are therefore not to be read as histories are, nevertheless a careful and critical study of them based on internal evidence sheds more light on the earliest times of Freemasonry than any other one source whatever. It is believed that the Old Charges were used in making a Mason in the old Operative days; that they served as constitutions of lodges in many cases, and sometimes functioned as what we today call a warrant.

The systematic study of these manuscripts began in the middle of the past century, at which time only a few were known to be in existence. In 1872 William James Hughan listed 32. Owing largely to his efforts many others were discovered, so that in 1889 Gould was able to list 62, and Hughan himself in 1895 tabulated 66 manuscript copies, 9 printed versions and 11 missing versions. This number has been so much increased of late years that in Ars Quatuor Coronatorum, Volume XXXI, page 40 (1918), Brother Roderick H. Baxter, now Worshipful Master of Quatuor Coronati Lodge, listed 98, which number included the versions known to be missing. Brother

Baxter's list is peculiarly valuable in that he gives data as to when and where these manuscripts have been reproduced.

For the sake of being better able to compare one copy with another, Dr. W. Begemann classified all the versions into four general "families", The Grand Lodge Family, The Sloane Family, The Roberts Family, and The Spencer Family. These family groups he divided further into branches, and he believed that The Spencer Family was an offshoot of The Grand Lodge Family, and The Roberts Family an offshoot of The Sloane Family. In this general manner of grouping, the erudite doctor was followed by Hughan, Gould and their colleagues, and his classification still holds in general; attempts have been made in recent years to upset it, but without much success. One of the best charts, based on Begemann, is that made by Brother Lionel Vibert, a copy of which will be published in a future issue of The Builder.

The first known printed reference to these Old Charges was made by Dr. Robert Plot in his Natural History of Staffordshire, published in 1686. Dr. A.F.A. Woodford and William James Hughan were the first to undertake a scientific study. Hughan's Old Charges is to this day the standard work in English. Gould's chapter in his History of Masonry would probably be ranked second in value, whereas the voluminous writings of Dr. Begemann, contributed by him to Zirkelcorrespondez, official organ of the National Grand Lodge of Germany, would, if only they were translated into English, give us the most exhaustive treatment of the subject ever yet written.

The Old Charges are peculiarly English. No such documents have ever been found in Ireland. Scotch manuscripts are known to be of English origin. It was once held by Findel and other German writers that the English versions ultimately derived from German sources, but this has been disproved. The only known point of similarity between the Old Charges and such German documents as the Torgau Ordinances and the Cologne Constitutions is the Legend of the Four Crowned Martyrs, and this legend is found among English versions only in the Regius Manuscript. As Gould well says, the British MSS. have "neither predecessors nor rivals"; they are the richest and rarest things in the whole field of masonic writings.

When the Old Charges are placed side by side it is immediately seen that in their account of the traditional history of the Craft they vary in a great many particulars, nevertheless they appear to have derived from some common origin, and in the main they tell the same tale, which is as interesting as a fairy story out of Grimm. Did the original of this traditional account come from some individual or was it born out of a floating tradition, like the folk tales of ancient people? Authorities differ much on this point. Begemann not only declared that the first version of the story originated with an individual, but even set out what he deemed to be the literary sources used by that Great Unknown. The doctor's arguments are powerful. On the other hand, others contend that the story began as a general vague oral tradition, and that this was in the course of time reduced to writing. In either event, why was the story ever written? In all probability an answer to that question will never be forth-coming, but W. Harry Rylands and others have been of the opinion that the first written versions were made in response to a general Writ for Return issued in 1388. Rylands' words may be quoted: "It appears to me not at all improbable that much, if not all, of the legendary history was composed in answer to the Writ for Returns issued to the guilds all over the country, in the twelfth year of Richard the Second, A.D. 1388." (A.Q.C. XVL page 1)

II. THE TWO OLDEST MANUSCRIPTS

In 1757 King George II presented to the British Museum a collection of some 12,000 volumes, the nucleus of which had been laid by King Henry VII and which came to be known as the Royal Library. Among these books was a rarely beautiful manuscript written by hand on 64 pages of vellum, about four by five inches in size, which a cataloger, David Casley, entered as No. 17 A-1 under the title, "A Poem of Moral Duties: here entitled Constitutiones Artis Gemetrie Secundem." It was not until Mr. J.O. Halliwell, F.R.S. (afterwards Halliwell-Phillipps), a non-Mason, chanced to make the discovery that the manuscript was known to be a masonic document. Mr. Phillipps read a paper on the manuscript before the Society of Antiquaries in 1839, and in the following year published a volume entitled Early History of Freemasonry in England (enlarged and revised in 1844), in which he incorporated a transcript of the document along with a few pages in facsimile. This important work will be found incorporated in the familiar Universal Masonic Library, the rusty sheepskin bindings of which strike the eyes on almost every masonic book shelf. This manuscript was known as "The Halliwell", or as "The Halliwell-Phillipps" until some fifty years atfterwards Gould rechristened it, in honour of the Royal Library in which it is found, the "Regius", and since then this has become the more familiar cognomen.

David Casley, a learned specialist in old manuscripts, dated the "Regius" as of the fourteenth century. E.A. Bond, another expert, dated it as of the middle of the fifteenth century. Dr. Kloss, the German specialist, placed it between 1427 and 1445. But the majority have agreed on 1390 as the most probable date. "It is impossible to arrive at absolute certainty on this point," says Hughan, whose Old Charges should be consulted, "save that it is not likely to be older than 1390, but may be some twenty years or so later." Dr. W. Begemann made a study of the document that has never been equalled for thoroughness, and arrived at a conclusion that may be given in his own words: it was written "towards the end of the 14th or at least quite at the beginning of the 15th century (not in Gloucester itself, as being too southerly, but) in the north of Gloucestershire or in the neighbouring north of Herefordshire, or even possibly in the south of Worcestershire." (A.Q.C. VII, page 35.)

In 1889 an exact facsimile of this famous manuscript was published in Volume I of the Antigrapha produced by the Quatuor Coronati Lodge of Research, and was edited by the then secretary of that lodge, George William Speth, himself a brilliant authority, who supplied a glossary that is indispensable to the amateur student. Along with it was published a commentary by R. F. Gould, one of the greatest of all his masonic papers, though it is exasperating in its rambling arrangement and general lack of conclusiveness.

The Regius Manuscript is the only one of all the versions to be written in meter, and may have been composed by a priest, if one may judge by certain internal evidences, though the point is disputed. There are some 800 lines in the poem, the strictly masonic portion coming to an end at line 576, after which begins what Hughan calls a "sermonette" on moral duties, in which there is quite a Roman Catholic vein with references to "the sins seven", "the sweet lady" (referring to the Virgin) and to holy water. There is no such specific Mariolatry in any other version of the Old Charges, though the great majority of them express loyalty to "Holy Church" and all of them, until Anderson's familiar version, are specifically Christian, so far as religion is concerned.

The author furnishes a list of fifteen "points" and fifteen "articles", all of which are quite specific instructions concerning the behaviour of a Craftsman: this portion is believed by many to have been the charges to an initiate as used in the author's period, and is therefore deemed the most important feature of the book as furnishing us a picture of the regulations of the Craft at that remote date. The Craft is described as having come into existence as an organized fraternity in "King Adelstoune's day", but in this the author contradicts himself, because he refers to things "written in old books" (I modernize spelling of quotations) and takes for granted a certain antiquity for the Masonry, which, as in all the Old Charges, is made synonymous with Geometry, a thing very different in those days from the abstract science over which we laboured during our school days.

The Regius Poem is evidently a book about Masonry, rather than a document of Masonry, and may very well have been written by a non-mason, though there is no way in which we can verify such theories, especially seeing that we know nothing about the document save what it has to tell us about itself, which is little.

In his Commentary on the Regius MS, R. F. Gould produced a paragraph that has ever since served as the pivot of a great debate. It reads as follows and refers to the "sermonette" portion which deals with "moral duties": "These rules of decorum read very curiously in the present age, but their inapplicability to the circumstances of the working masons of the fourteen or fifteenth century will be at once apparent. They were intended for the gentlemen of those days, and the instruction for behaviour in the presence of a lord-at table and in the society of ladies-would have all been equally out of place in a code of manners drawn up for the use of a Guild or Craft of Artisans."

The point of this is that there must have been present among the Craftsmen of that time a number of men not engaged at all in labour, and therefore were, as we would now describe them, "speculatives." This would be of immense importance if Gould had made good his point, but that he was not able to do. The greatest minds of the period in question were devoted to architecture, and there is no reason not to believe that among the Craftsmen were members of good families. Also the Craft was in contact with the clergy all the while, and therefore many of its members may well have stood in need of rules for preserving proper decorum in great houses and among the members of the upper classes. From Woodford until the present time the great majority of masonic scholars have believed the Old Charges to have been used by a strictly operative craft and it is evident that they will continue to do so until more conclusive evidence to the contrary is forthcoming than Gould's surmise.

Next to the Regius the oldest manuscript is that known as the Cooke. It was published by R. Spencer, London, 1861 and was edited by Mr. Matthew Cooke, hence his name. In the British Museum's catalogue it is listed as "Additional M.S. 23,198", and has been dated by Hughan at 1450 or thereabouts, an estimate in which most of the specialists have concurred. Dr. Begemann believed the document to have been "compiled and written in the southeastern portion of the western Midlands, say, in Gloucestershire or Oxfordshire, possibly also in southeast Worcestershire or southwest Warwickshire. The 'Book of Charges' which forms the second part of the document is certainly of the 14th century, the historical or first part, of quite the beginning of the 15th." (A.Q.C. IX, page 18)

The Cooke MS. was most certainly in the hands of Mr. George Payne, when in his second term as Grand Master in 1720 he compiled the "General Regulations", and which Anderson included in his own version of the Constitutions published in 1723. Anderson himself evidently made use of lines 901-960 of the MS.

The Lodge Quatuor Coronati reprinted the Cooke in facsimile in Vol. II of its Antigrapha in 1890, and included therewith a Commentary by George William Speth which is, in my own amateur opinion, an even more brilliant piece of work than Gould's

Commentary on the Regius. Some of Speth's conclusions are of permanent value. I paraphrase his findings in my own words:

The M.S. is a transcript of a yet older document and was written by a mason. There were several versions of the Charges to a Mason in circulation at the time. The MS. is in two parts, the former of which is an attempt at a history of the Craft, the latter of which is a version of the Charges. Of this portion Speth writes that it is "far and away the earliest, best and purest version of the 'Old Charges' which we possess." The MS. mentions nine "articles", and these evidently were legal enforcements at the time; the nine "points" given were probably not legally binding but were morally so. "Congregations" of Masons were held here and there but no "General Assembly" (or "Grand Lodge"); Grand Masters existed in fact but not in name and presided at one meeting of a congregation only. "Many of our present usages may be traced in their original form to this manuscript."

III. ANDERSON's CONSTITUTIONS AND OTHER PRINTED VERSIONS

One of the most important of all the versions of the Old Charges is not an ancient original at all, but a printed edition issued in 1722, and known as the Roberts, though it is believed to be a copy of an ancient document. Of this W. J. Hughan writes: "The only copy known was purchased by me at Brother Spencer's sale of masonic works, etc. (London, 1875), for 8 pounds 10s., on behalf of the late Brother R. F. Bower, and is now in the magnificent library of the Grand Lodge of Iowa, U.S.A." This tiny volume is easily the most priceless masonic literary possession in America, and was published in exact facsimile by the National masonic Research Society, with an eloquent Introduction by Dr. Joseph Fort Newton in 1916. The Reverend Edmund Coxe edited a famous reprint in 1871. It is a version meriting the most careful study on the part of the masonic student because it had a decided influence on the literature and jurisprudence of the Craft after its initial appearance. It appeared in one of the most interesting and momentous periods of modern Speculative Masonry, namely, in the years between the organization of the first Grand Lodge in 1717 and the appearance of Anderson's Constitution in 1723. It is the earliest printed version of the Old Charges known to exist.

Another well-known printed version is that published in 1724 and known as the Briscoe. This was the second publication of its kind. The third printed version was issued in 1728-9 by Benjamin Cole, and known as the Cole Edition in consequence. This version is considered a literary gem in that the main body of the text is engraved throughout in most beautiful style. A special edition of this book was made in Leeds, 1897, the value of which was enhanced by one of W. J. Hughan's famous introductions. For our own modern and practical purposes the most important of all the versions ever made was that compiled by Dr. James Anderson in 1723 and everywhere known familiarly as Anderson's Constitution. A second edition appeared, much changed and enlarged, in 1738; a third, by John Entick, in 1756; and so on every few years until by 1888 twenty-two editions in all had been issued. The Rev. A.F.A. Woodford, Hughan's collaborator, edited an edition of The Constitution Book of 1723 as Volume I of Kenning's masonic Archeological Library, under date of 1878. This is a correct and detailed reproduction of the book exactly as Anderson first published it, and is valuable accordingly.

Anderson's title page is interesting to read: "The CONSTITUTION, History, Laws, Charges, Orders, Regulations, and Usages, of the Right Worshipful FRATERNITY of ACCEPTED FREE MASONS; collected from their general RECORDS, and their faithful TRADITIONS of many Ages. To be read At the Admission of a NEW BROTHER, when the Master or Warden shall begin, or order some other Brother to read as follows, etc." After the word "follows" Anderson's own version of masonic history begins with this astonishing statement:

"Adam, our first Parent, created after the Image of God, the great Architect of the Universe, must have had the Liberal Sciences, particularly Geometry, written on his Heart, etc."

Thus did Dr. Anderson launch his now thrice familiar account of the history of Freemasonry, an account which, save in the hands of the most expert masonic antiquarian, yields very little dependable historical fact whatsoever, but which, owing to the prestige of its author, came to be accepted for generations as a bona fide history of the Craft. It will be many a long year yet before the rank and file of brethren shall have learned that Dr. Anderson's "history" belongs in the realm of fable for the most part, and has never been accepted as anything else by knowing ones.

The established facts concerning Dr. Anderson's own private history comprise a record almost as brief as the short and simple annals of the poor. Brother J.T. Thorp, one of the most distinguished of the veterans among living English masonic scholars, has given it in an excellent brief form. (A.Q.C. XVIII, page 9.)

"Of this distinguished Brother we know very little. He is believed to have been born, educated and made a Mason in Scotland, subsequently settling in London as a Presbyterian Minister. He is mentioned for the first time in the Proceedings of the Grand Lodge of England on September 29th, 1721, when he was appointed to revise the old Gothic Constitutions-this revision was approved by the Grand Lodge of England on September 29th in 1723, in which year Anderson was Junior Grand Warden under the Duke of Wharton-he published a second edition of the Book of Constitutions in 1738, and died in 1739. This is about all that is known of him."

In his 1738 edition Anderson so garbled up his account of the founding of Grand Lodge, and contradicted his own earlier story in such fashion, that R. F. Gould was inclined to believe either that he had become disgruntled and full of spleen, or else that he was in his dotage. Be that as it may, Anderson's historical pages are to be read with extreme caution. His Constitution itself, or that part dealing with the principles and regulations of the Craft, is most certainly a compilation made of extracts of other versions of the Old Charges pretty much mixed with the Doctor's own ideas in the premises, and so much at variance with previous customs that the official adoption thereof caused much dissension among the lodges, and may have had something to do with the disaffection which at last led to the formation of the "Antient" Grand Lodge of 1751 or thereabouts. The "Anderson" of this latter body, which in time waxed very powerful, was Laurence Dermott, a brilliant Irishman, who as Grand Secretary was leader of the "Antient" forces for many years, and who wrote for the body its own Constitution, called Ahiman Rezon, which cryptic title is believed by some to mean "Worthy Brother Secretary." The first edition of this important version was made in 1756, a second in 1764, and so on until by 1813 an eighth had been published. A very complete collection of all editions is in the masonic Library at Philadelphia. A few of our Grand Lodges, Pennsylvania among them, continue to call their Book of Constitutions, The Ahiman Rezon.

Anderson himself is still on the rack of criticism. Learned brethren are checking this, sifting through pages and leaving no stone unturned in order to appraise correctly his contributions to masonic history. But there is not so much disagreement on the Constitution. In that document, which did not give satisfaction to many upon its appearance, Anderson, as Brother Lionel Vibert has well said, "builded better than he knew," because he produced a document which until now serves as the groundwork of nearly all Grand Lodge Constitutions having jurisdiction over Symbolic Masonry, and which once and for all established Speculative Freemasonry on a basis apart, and with no sectarian character, either as to religion or politics. For all his faults as a historian (and these faults were as much of his age as of his own shortcomings), Anderson is a great figure in our annals and deserves at the hand of every student a careful and, reverent study.

IV. CONCLUSION

In concluding this very brief and inconclusive sketch of a great subject, I return to my first statement. In the whole circle of masonic studies there is not, for us Americans at any rate, any subject of such importance as this of the Old Charges, especially insofar as they have to do with our own Constitutions and Regulations, and that is very much indeed. Many false conceptions of Freemasonry may be directly traced to an unlearned, or wilful misinterpretation of the Old Charges, what they are, what they mean to us, and what their authority may be. In this land jurisprudence is a problem of supreme importance, and in a way not very well comprehended by our brethren in other parts, who often wonder why we should be so obsessed by it. We have forty-nine Grand Lodges, each of which is sovereign in its own state, and all of which must maintain fraternal relations with scores of Grand bodies abroad as well as with each other. These Grand Lodges assemble each year to legislate for the Craft, and therefore, in the very nature of things, the organization and government of the Order is for us Americans a much more complicated and important thing than it can be in other lands. To know what the Old Charges are, and to understand masonic constitutional law and practice, is for our leaders and law-givers a prime necessity.

WORKS CONSULTED IN PREPARING THIS ARTICLE

Gould's History of Freemasonry, Vol. 1, beginning on page 56; A.Q.C., I, 127; A.Q.C., I, 147; A.Q.C., I, 152; A.Q.C., IV, 73; A.Q.C., IV, 83; A.Q.C., IV, 171; A.Q.C., V, 37; A.Q.C., IV, 201; A.Q.C, IV, 36,198; A.Q.C., VII, 119; A.Q.C., VIII, 224; Hughan, Old Charges; A.Q.C., IX, 18; A.Q.C., IX, 85; A.Q.C., XI, 205; A.Q.C., XIV, 153; A.Q.C., XVI, 4; A.Q.C., XVIII, 16; A.Q.C., XX, 249; A.Q.C., XXI, 161, 211; A.Q.C., XXVIII, 189; Gould's Concise History, chapter V; Gould, Collected Essays, 3; Stillson, History of Freemasonry and Concordant Orders, 157; A.Q.C., XXXIII, 5; The masonic Review, Vol. XIII, 297; Edward Conder, Records of the Hole Craft and Fellowship of Masons; Vibert, Story of the Craft; Vibert, Freemasonry Before the Era of Grand Lodge; Findel, History of Freemasonry; Hughan, Cole's Constitutions; Fort, Early History and Antiquities of Freemasonry; Pierson, Traditions, Origin and Early History of Freemasonry; Hughan, Ancient masonic Rolls: Waite, New Encyclopedia of Freemasonry; Clegg, Mackey's Revised History; Ward, Freemasonry and the Ancient Gods: A.Q.C., Antigapha, all volumes.

THE OLD CHARGES AND WHAT THEY MEAN TO US

Supplementary References: Mackey's Encyclopedia (Revised Edition). Ahiman Rezon, 37; Antients, 55; Ars Quatuor Coronatorum, 80; Arts, 80; Benjamin Cole, 157; Charges of 1722, 143; Congregations, 174; Cooke's Manuscript, 178; Dr. James Anderson, 57; Dr. Robert Plot, 570; Four Crowned Martyrs, 272; George B.F. Kloss, 383; Gothic Constitutions, 304; Halliwell Manuscript, 316; John Entick, 246; Laurence Dermott, 206; Legend, 433; Legend of the Craft, 434; Old Charges, 143; Old Manuscripts, 464; Old Records, 612; Old Regulations, 527; Operative Masonry, 532; Parts, 544; Plot Manuscript, 569; Points, 572; Regius Manuscript, 616; Roberts' Manuscript, 627; Speculative Masonry, 704.

THE

Old Conſtitutions,

Belonging to the

Ancient *and* Honourable

SOCIETY

OF

Free *and* Accepted

MASONS.

Taken from a Manuſcript wrote above Five
Hundred Years ſince.

LONDON;

Printed, and Sold by J. ROBERTS, in
Warwick-Lane, MDCCXXII.

(Price Six-Pence.)

Robert's Constitutions (1722)
The Old Constitutions
Belonging to the Ancient and Honourable Society of Free and Accepted Masons.

Taken from a Manuscript wrote above Five Hundred Years since.
London:
Printed and sold by J. Roberts, in *Warwick-Lane*, MDCCXXII. (Price Six-Pence.)

The Preface

If any Thing could have escaped the Censures of this litigious Age; if the most innocent inoffensive Set of Men in the World could be free from Satyr and Sarcasm, one would have thought the Ancient and Noble Society of Free-Masons should have been the Men. What have they not to recommend them to the World, and gain the Favour and Protection of wise and honest Men?

As their Art is the most Ancient, so their Profession of it is most Honourable. The Necessity the World was early in of the Profession of a Mason, proves their Usefulness; for I believe it will not be doubted, that Men had Houses before they had Cloaths, as they had Altars before they had Temples. Cain built a City, and Abel, no doubt, built an Altar, when he offered his Sacrifice to the LORD.

THUS useful, and thus ancient, it cannot be wondered if the World honour'd them with all the Tokens of Respect, which in those Days they were capable of, and perhaps more than we have yet an Account of.

THESE Honours, and this Respect, it cannot be doubted brought Men of Value among them, who thought it not below them to wear the Badge of the Society, and to acknowledge themselves to be Favourers of their Greatness, as they were Lovers of Art.

UNDER the Protection of such Persons of Honour and Interest, it is not to be express'd what mighty Fabricks they have erected, what glorious Buildings they have rais'd, from the Temple of Solomon to the magnificent Pile of St. Peter's at Rome.

HOW this Society has been preserv'd; How regularly they have acted; on what wholesome Laws they have been founded, and how carefully they have observ'd and regarded those Laws, as the just

Cement of the Society, that is partly to be seen in this Tract, and it will speak for itself.

NOR is their Value lessen'd or abated at all by the Dust and Scandal rais'd by any Men against them, or by the freedom they have taken to banter and rally them. The Dirt thrown at them flies back on those that cast it, and the Honour of the Society of Free-Masons remains entire. So that none of the Persons of Honour who have lately grac'd the Society with their Presence, have yet seen any Reason to be asham'd of them, or to withdraw their Protection from them.

MUCH more might be said to their Honour, but the following Piece of Antiquity is sufficient, and will give every Reader an Authentick Account of them. It has yet seen the World but in Fragments, but is now put together as a Thing of too much Significancy to pass our Observation, and which will effectually vindicate the Ancient Society of Free-Masons from all that has or can be said against them.

The History of Free Masons, &c.

THE Almighty Father of Heaven, with the Wisdom of the Glorious Son, thro' the Goodness of the Holy Ghost, Three Persons in one Godhead, be with our Beginning, and give us his grace so to govern our Lives, that we may come to his Bliss, that never shall have end. Amen.

GOOD Brethren and Fellows, our Purpose is to tell you how, and in what manner the Craft of *Masonry* was begun, and afterwards how it was founded by worthy Kings and Princes, and other wise Men, hurtful to none, and also to them that be true, we will declare doth belong to every Free Mason to keep firm good Faith, if you take Heed thereunto it is well worthy to be kept, which is contain'd in the Seven Liberal Sciences as follows, viz.

Imprimis, It's *Grammar* that teaches a Man to speak truly, and write truly

II. - It's *Rhetorick* that teaches a Man to speak fair, and in subtle Terms.

III. - It's *Logick* that teaches a Man to discern truth from Falshood.

IV. - It's *Arithmetick* that teaches a Man to Accompt, and reckon all manner of Numbers.

V. - It's *Geometry* that teaches Mett and Measure of any Thing, and from thence cometh *Masonry*.

VI. - It's *Musick* that teacheth Song and Voice.

VII. - It's *Astronomy* which teacheth to know the Course of the Sun, Moon, and other Ornaments of Heaven.

Note, I pray you, That these Seven are contain'd under *Geometry*, for it teacheth Mett and Measure, Ponderation and Weight for every Thing in and upon the whole Earth for you to know; that every Craftsman works by Measure; He or she that buys or sells, is by Weight or Measure; Husbandmen, Navigators, Planters, and all of them, use *Geometry*; for neither *Grammar*, *Rhetorick*, *Logick*, nor any other of the said Sciences can subsist without *Geometry*, *ergo*, most worthy and honourable.

You ask me how this Science was invented; my Answer is this, That before the General Deluge, which is commonly called *Noah's* Flood, there was a Man called *Lamech*, as you may read in the Fourth Chapter of *Genesis*, who had two Wives, the one called *Ada*, the other *Zilla*; by *Ada* he begat two Sons, *Jabal* and *Jubal*; by *Zilla* he had one Son called *Tubal*, and a Daughter called *Naamah*. These four Children found the beginning of all Crafts in the World: *Jabal* found out *Geometry*, and he divided Flocks of Sheep, and Lands; he first built a House of Stone and Timber. *Jubal* found out *Musick*; *Tubal* found out the Smith's Trade or Craft, also of Gold, Silver, Copper, Iron and Steel; *Naamah* found out the Craft of Weaving.

And these children knew that GOD would take Vengeance for Sins, either by Fire or Water, wherefore they did write these Sciences, that they had found, on two Pillars of Stone, that they might be found after that GOD had taken Vengeance; the one was *Marble*, that would not burn, the other was *Latress*, that would not drown in Water; so that the one would be preserved, and not consumed, if GOD would any People should live upon the Earth.

It resteth now to tell you how these Stones were found, whereon the said Sciences were written, after the said Deluge: It so pleased God Almighty, that the Great *Hermarmes*, whose Son *Lunie* was, who was the son of Sem, who was the son of Noah. The said *Hermarmes* was afterwards called *Hermes*, the Father of *Lunie*, he found one of the two Pillars of Stone. He found these Sciences written thereon, and taught them to other Men. And at the Tower of *Babylon*, *Masonry* was much made on; for the King of *Babylon*, who was *Nemorth*, was a

Mason, and serv'd the Science; and when the City of *Ninevah*, and other Cities of the *East*, should be built, *Nemorth* sent there threescore Masons, at the Desire of the King of *Ninevah*; and when they went forth, he gave them a Charge after this manner, That they should be true one to another, and love one another, that he might have Worship by them in sending them to his Cozen the King. He also gave them Charge concerning their Science; and then it was the first time that any *Mason* had Charge of his Work. Also *Abraham*, and *Sarah* his Wife, went into *Egypt*, and taught the *Egyptians* the Seven Liberal Sciences; and he had an ingenious Schollar called *Euclydes*, who perfectly learned the said Liberal Sciences.

It happen'd in his Days, the Lords and States of the Realm had so many Sons unlawfully begotten by other Men's Wives, that the Land was burthen'd with them, having small Means to maintain them withal; the King understanding thereof, caused a Parliament to be called or summoned for Redress, but being so Numberless that no Good could be done with them, he caused Proclamation to be made through the Realm, that if any Man could devise any Course how to maintain them, to inform the King, and he should be well rewarded; whereupon *Euclydes* came to the King, and said thus, My noble Sovereign, if I may have the Order of Government of those Lords' Sons, I will teach them the Seven Liberal Sciences, whereby they may live honestly like Gentlemen, provided that you will grant me Power over them by virtue of your Dominion; which was immediately effected, and there *Euclydes* gave them these Admonitions following

I. - To be true to their King.

II. -To be true to the Master they serve.

III. - To be true, and love one another.

IV. - Not to miscall one another, &c.

V. - To do their Work so duly, that they may deserve their Wages at their Master's Hands.

VI. - To ordain the wisest of them Master of the rest of the Work.

VII. - To have such reasonable Wages, that the Workman may live honestly, and with Credit.

VIII. - To come and assemble together in the Year, to take Council in their Craft how they may work best to serve their Lord and Master, for his Profit, and their own Credit, and to correct such as have offended.

Note, that *Masonry* was heretofore term'd *Geometry*, and sithence the Children of *Israel* came to the Land of *Bethest*, which is now called *Emens*, in the Country of *Jerusalem*, where they began a Temple, which is now called the Temple of *Jerusalem*: And King *David* loved *Masons* well and cherish'd them, for he gave them good Payment, and gave them a Charge, as *Euclydes* had given them before in *Egypt*, and further, as hereafter followeth; and after the Decease of King *David*, *Solomon* his Son finished the Temple that his Father had began; he sent for *Masons* of divers Nations, to the Number of Four and Twenty Thousand, of which Number Four Thousand were elected and created Masters and Governors of the Work. And there was a King of another Region or Country, called *Hiram*, who loved well King *Solomon*, and he gave him Timber for the Work; and he had a Son called *Amon*, and he was Master of *Geometry*, and he was chief Master of all his *Masons* of Carving-Work, and of all other Work of *Masonry* that belong'd to the Temple, as appears by the Bible in *Lib. Regum Cap. 4*. And King *Solomon* confirmed all Things concerning *Masons*, that *David* his Father had given in Charge; and then *Masons* did travel divers Countries, some to augment their Knowledge in the said Art, and to instruct others.

And it happen'd that a curious *Mason* named *Memongrecus*, that had been at the building of *Solomon's* Temple, came into *France*, and taught the Science of *Masonry* to the *Frenchmen*; and there was a King of *France* called *Carolus Martel*, who loved greatly *Masonry*, who sent for the said *Memongrecus*, and learned of him the said Sciences, and became one of the Fraternity; and thereupon began great Works, and liberally did pay his Workmen: He confirm'd unto them a large Charter, and was yearly present at their Assembly, which was a great Honour and Encouragement unto them; and thus came the Science into *France*.

The Knowledge of *Masonry* was unknown in *England* until St. *Alban* came thither, who instructed the King in the said Science of *Masonry*, and also in Divinity, who was a *Pagan*: He walled the Town now called St. *Alban*; he became in high Favour with the King, insomuch that he was Knighted, and made the King's Chief Steward, and the Realm was governed by him under the said King. He greatly cherished and loved *Masons*, and truly paid them their Wages Weekly, which was 3 *s*. 6 *d*. the Week. He also purchased for them a Charter from the King to hold a General Assembly and Council Yearly. He made many *Masons* and gave them such a Charge as is hereafter declared.

It happen'd presently after the Martyrdom of St. *Alban*, who is truly term'd *England's Proto-Martyr*, that a certain King invaded the Land, and destroy'd most of the Natives by Fire and Sword, that the Science of *Masonry* was much decay'd, until the Reign of King *Athelston*, which some write *Adleston*, who brought the Land to Peace and Rest, from the insulting *Danes*. He began to build many Abbies, Monasteries, and other Religious Houses, as also Castles and divers Fortresses for Defence of his Realm. He loved *Masons* more than his Father; he greatly study'd *Geometry*, and sent into many Lands for Men expert in the Science. He gave them a very large Charter, to hold a Yearly Assembly, and Power to correct Offenders in the said Science; and the King himself caused a General Assembly of all *Masons* in his Realm, at *York*, and there made many *Masons*, and gave them a deep Charge for Observation of all such Articles as belonged unto *Masonry*, and delivered them the said Charter to keep; and when this Assembly was gathered together, he caused a Cry to be made, that if any of them had any Writing that did concern *Masonry*, or could inform the King of any Thing or Matter that was wanting in the said Charge already delivered, that they or he should shew them to the King, or recite them to him; and there were some in *French*, some in *Greek*, and some in *English*, and other Languages, whereupon the King caused a Book to be made, which declared how the Science was first invented, and the Utility thereof, which Book he commanded to be read, and plainly declared, when any Man was to be made a *Mason* that he might fully understand what Articles, Rules and Orders he was obliged to observe; and from that time unto this Day *Masonry* hath been much respected and preserved, and divers new Articles have been added to the said Charge, by good Advice and Consent of the Masters and Fellows.

Tunc Unus ex Senioribus veniat librum illi qui Injurandum reddat & ponat Manum in libro vel supra librum dum Articulus & Precepta sibi legentur.

Saying thus by way of Exhortation,

MY loving and respected Friends and Brethren, I humbly beseech you, as you love your Soul's eternal Welfare, your Credit, and your Country's Good, to be very Careful in Observation of these Articles that I am about to read to this Deponent; for ye are obliged to perform them as well as he, so hoping of your Care herein, I will, by God's Grace, begin the Charge.

I. - I am to admonish you to honour God in his holy Church; that, you use no Heresy, Schism and Error in your Understandings, or discredit Men's Teachings.

II. - To be true to our Sovereign Lord the King, his Heirs and lawful Successors; committing no Treason, Misprision of Treason, or Felony; and if any Man shall commit Treason that you know of, you shall forthwith give Notice thereof to his Majesty, his Privy Counsellors, or some other Person that hath Commission to enquire thereof.

III. - You shall be true to your Fellows and Brethren of the Science of Masonry, and do unto them as you would be done unto.

IV. - You shall keep Secret the obscure and intricate Parts of the Science, not disclosing them to any but such as study and use the same.

V. - You shall do your Work truly and faithfully, endeavouring the Profit and Advantage of him that is Owner of the said Work.

VI. - You shall call Masons your Fellows and Brethren, without Addition of Knaves, or other bad Language.

VII. - You shall not take your Neighbour's Wife Willinously, nor his Daughter, nor his Maid or his Servant, to use ungodly.

VIII. - You shall not carnally lye with any Woman that is belonging to the House where you are at Table.

IX. - You shall truly pay for your Meat and Drink, where you are at Table.

X. - You shall not undertake any Man's Work, knowing yourself unable or unexpert to perform and effect the same, that no Discredit or Aspersion may be imputed to the Science, or the Lord or Owner of the said Work be any wise prejudic'd.

XI. - You shall not take any Work to do at excessive or unreasonable Rates, to deceive the Owner thereof, but so as he may be truly and faithfully serv'd with his own Goods.

XII. - You shall so take your Work, that thereby you may live honestly, and pay your Fellows the Wages as the Science doth require.

XIII. - You shall not supplant any of your Fellows of their Work, (that is to say) if he or any of them hath or have taken any Work upon him or them, or he or they stand Master or Masters of any Lord or Owner's Work, that you shall not put him or them out from the said Work, altho' you perceive him or them unable to finish the same.

XIV. - You shall not take any Apprentice to serve you in the said Science of *Masonry*, under the Term of Seven Years; nor any but such as are descended of good and honest Parentage, that no Scandal may be imputed to the said Science of *Masonry*.

XV. - You shall not take upon you to make any one *Mason* without the Privity or Consent of six, or five at least of your Fellows, and not but such as is Freeborn, and whose Parents live in good Fame and Name, and that hath his right and perfect Limbs, and able of Body to attend the said Science.

XVI. - You shall not pay any of your Fellows more Money than he or they have deserv'd, that you be not deceiv'd by slight or false Working, and the Owner thereof much wrong'd.

XVII. - You shall not slander any of your Fellows behind their Backs, to impair their Temporal Estate or good Name.

XVIII. - You shall not, without very urgent Cause, answer your Fellow doggedly or ungodly, but as becomes a loving Brother in the said Science.

XIX. - You shall duly reverence your Fellows, that the Bond of Charity and mutual Love may continue stedfast and stable amongst you.

XX. - You shall not (except in *Christmas* time) use any lawless Games, as Dice, Cards, or such like.

XXI. - You shall not frequent any Houses of Bawdery, or be a Pander to any of your Fellows or others, which will be a great Scandal to the Science.

XXII. - You shall not go out to drink by Night, or if Occasion happen that you must go, you shall not stay past Eight of the Clock, having some of your Fellows, or one at the least, to bear you Witness of the honest Place you were in, and your good Behaviour, to avoid Scandal.

XXIII. - You shall come to the Yearly Assembly, if you know where it is kept, being within Ten Miles of the Place of your Abode, submitting your self to the Censure of your Fellows, wherein you have .... to make satisfaction, or else to defend by Order of the King's Laws.

XXIV. - You shall not make any Mould, Square, or Rule to mould Stones withal, but such as are allowed by the Fraternity.

XXV. - You shall set Strangers at Work, having Employment for them, at least a Fortnight, and pay them their Wages truly, and if you want Work for them, then you shall relieve them with Money to defray their reasonable Charges to the next Lodge.

XXVI. - You shall truly attend your Work, and truly end the same, whether it be Task or Journey-Work, if you may have the Payment and Wages according to your Agreement made with the Master or Owner thereof.

All these Articles and Charge, which I have now read unto you, you shall well and truly observe, perform and keep to the best of your Power, and Knowledge, So help you God, and the true and holy Contents of this Book.

And moreover I A. B. do here in the Presence of God Almighty and of my Fellows and Brethren here present, promise and declare, That I will not at any Time hereafter by any Act or Circumstance whatsoever, directly or indirectly, publish, discover, reveal or make known any of these Secrets, Privities or Councils of the Fraternity or Fellowship of Free-Masons, which at this time, or at any time hereafter shall be made known unto me.

So help me God, and the true and holy Contents of this Book.

This Charge belongeth to Apprentices.

Imprimis. - YOU shall truly honour God, and his holy Church, the King, your Master, and Dame; you shall not absent yourself, but with the Licence of one or both of them, from their Service, by Day or Night.

II. - You shall not Purloyn or Steal, or be Privy or accessary to the Purloyning or Stealing to the Value of Six-pence from them or either of them.

III. - You shall not commit Adultery or Fornication in the House of your Master, with his Wife, Daughter or Maid.

IV. - You shall not disclose your Master's or Dame's Secrets or Councils, which they have reported unto you, or what is to be concealed, spoken or done within the Privities of their House, by them, or either of them, or by any *Free-Mason*.

V. - You shall not maintain any disobedient Argument with your Master, Dame, or any *Free-Mason*.

VI. - You shall reverently behave your self towards all *Free-Masons*, using neither Cards, Dice, or any other unlawful Games, *Christmas* Time excepted.

VII. - You shall not haunt, or frequent any Taverns or Ale-houses, or so much as go into any of them, except it be upon your Master or your Dame, their or any of their Affairs, or with their or the one of their Consents.

VIII. - You shall not commit Adultery or Fornication in any Man's House, where you shall be at Table or at Work.

IX. - You shall not marry, or contract yourself to any Woman during your Apprenticeship.

X. - You shall not steal any Man's Goods, but especially your Master's, or any of his Fellow *Masons*, nor suffer any to steal their Goods, but shall hinder the Felon, if you can; and if you cannot, then you shall acquaint the said Master and his Fellows presently.

Additional Orders and Constitutions
Made and agreed upon at a General Assembly held at ....,
on the Eighth Day of December, 1663.

I. - THAT no Person, of what Degree soever, be accepted a *Free-Mason*, unless he shall have a Lodge of five *Free-Masons* at the least, whereof one to be a Master or Warden of that Limit or Division where such Lodge shall be kept, and another to be a Workman of the Trade of *Free-Masonry*.

II. - That no Person hereafter shall be accepted a *Free-Mason*, but such as are of able Body, honest Parentage, good Reputation, and Observers of the Laws of the Land.

III. - That no Person hereafter, which shall be accepted a *Free-Mason*, shall be admitted into any Lodge, or Assembly, until he hath brought a Certificate of the Time and Place of his Acception, from the Lodge that accepted him, unto the Master of that Limit and Division, where such Lodge was kept, which said Master shall enroll the same on Parchment in a Roll to be kept for that Purpose, and give an Account of all such Acceptions, at every General Assembly.

IV. - That every Person, who is now a *Free-Mason*, shall bring to the Master a Note of the Time of his Acception, to the end the same may be enrolled in such Priority of Place, as the Person deserves, and to the end the whole Company and Fellows may the better know each other.

V. - That for the future the said Society, Company and Fraternity of *Free-Masons*, shall be regulated and governed by one Master, and as many Wardens as the said Company shall think fit to chuse at every Yearly General Assembly.

VI. - That no Person shall be accepted a *Free-Mason*, unless he be One and Twenty Years Old, or more.

VII. - That no person hereafter be accepted a *Free-Mason*, or know the Secrets of the said Society, until he shall have first taken the Oath of Secrecy here following, viz.

I *A. B.* do here in the Presence of God Almighty, and of my Fellows and Bretheren here present, promise and declare, That I will not at any Time hereafter by any Act or Circumstance whatsoever directly or indirectly, publish, discover, reveal or make known any of the Secrets, Privities or Councils of the Fraternity or Fellowship of Free Masons, which at this time, or at any time hereafter shall be made known unto me.

So help me God, and the true and holy Contents of this Book.

FINIS.

ORDO AB CHAO.

AD UNIVERSI TERRARUM ORBIS SUMMI ARCHITECTI GLORIAM.

DEUS MEUMQUE JUS.

PROCEEDINGS

OF THE

ANNUAL SESSION

OF THE

SUPREME COUNCIL

OF

Sovereign Grand Inspectors General,

33d and Last Degree of the Ancient and Accepted Rite,

FOR THE SOUTHERN JURISDICTION OF THE U. S. A.

HELD AT THE VALLEY OF NEW ORLEANS,

On the 20th, 21st and 22d days of the month called "Sebat," A∴ M∴ 5617, corresponding to the 14th, 15th and 17th days of February, in the Vulgar Era, 1847.

NEW ORLEANS:
PRINTED AT THE BULLETIN BOOK AND JOB OFFICE.
1857.

The Supreme Council Session in New Orleans
Michael R. Poll, P.M.
Secretary, Louisiana Lodge of Research

When talking about the Scottish Rite, two of the most popular questions asked are when did Albert Pike receive his 33° and where. The answers can be found in the Southern Jurisdiction's rare 1857 Proceedings (reproduced follow). The short answer is that he received the 33° on April 25th 1857, "in the Grand Lodge Hall, corner of St. Charles and Perdido streets, City of New Orleans, state of Louisiana." As so often is the case when studying historical events, the short answer hardly tells the whole story.

From just this one amazing book, we can pick up a number of interesting facts. The degree took place just two years following the Concordat of 1855 between the Supreme Council, Southern Jurisdiction, USA (Charleston Supreme Council) and the Supreme Council of Louisiana — or, really, about half of it. The Concordat of 1855 was an attempt to unify or bring together the supreme councils at Charleston and New Orleans. It was not wholly successful and only about half of the 33rds in New Orleans agreed to participate. What followed was an unfortunate and damaging period of conflict.

At the time of these Proceedings, the Southern Jurisdiction followed the *Grand Constitutions of 1786* as their "rules of order" for the governing of the supreme council. Article V of these *Constitutions* states that "Every Supreme Council will consist of nine Grand Inspectors General of the 33d degree ...". Accordingly, the Southern Jurisdiction had no more than 9 Sovereign Grand Inspectors General as its Active Members. The Supreme Council of Louisiana, however, had changed their rules several years earlier and expanded their council to 33 Active Members. It would not be until the time of Albert Pike as Sovereign Grand Commander that the Southern Jurisdiction would expand the number of its Active Members to 33. The result was that at the time of the Concordat, (and with only about *half* of the Active Members of the Supreme Council of Louisiana participating), the 33rds formerly under the Supreme Council of Louisiana outnumbered the 33rds in the Southern Jurisdiction. When the time came to bring everyone together, the Southern Jurisdiction simply could not accommodate all of these additional 33rds as Active Members.

In the summer of 1856, Albert Mackey would offer the first available Active Membership following the Concordat (as well as head of the Grand Consistory of Louisiana) to former Supreme Council of Louisiana Sovereign Grand Commander, James Foulhouze. Upon Foulhouze's refusal, the Active Membership would be offered to, and accepted by, Claude Samory. Leadership of the Grand Consistory of Louisiana would soon pass to a relatively new Scottish Rite Mason by the name of Albert Pike.

In an attempt to somehow find a place for the former Active Members of the Supreme Council of Louisiana who participated in the Concordat, the Southern Jurisdiction created what became known as the "Chamber of Deputies" consisting of 9 former Active Members of the Supreme Council of Louisiana. The members of this chamber would serve as Deputies of the Southern Jurisdiction. You will note on page 33 of the 1857 Proceedings that it was the Deputies (with the blessing of Albert Mackey) who elected Albert Pike to receive the 33°. You will also note that at the 1857 Session the only Active Member present was Claude Samory. In fact, every 33rd listed as attending was a former Active Member of the Supreme Council of Louisiana. That's right, Albert Pike received his 33° from 33rds formerly under the Supreme Council of Louisiana. Claude Samory was, at the time of the Concordat, the Lt. Grand Commander of the Supreme Council of Louisiana, Charles Claiborne, the Sovereign Grand Commander and Charles Laffon de Ladebat (who gave up his seat in the "Chamber of Deputies" in favor of Albert Pike) was the Secretary General.

When we look at days long gone, we sometimes apply today's customs and practices to the past. This will often lead us into misunderstandings. The way things are done today offers no guarantee that this was the practice long ago. Today, the term "Illustrious Brother" is reserved for those who have received the 33°. You will note in the image of page 33 that Albert Pike and Willis P. Coleman, both (at the time) 32nds are given the title "Illustrious." This is because in the 1800's the term "Illustrious" applied to both

32nds and 33rds. A 32nd was considered to be one of considerable rank and standing. You will also note that there is no mention of anyone being a Knight Commander of the Court of Honour. This is because the KCCH as well as the Grand Cross of the Court of Honour investitures were not invented at that time. It would not be until Albert Pike became Sovereign Grand Commander and after his seeing and obtaining the ritual of the old *Ceremony of the Fiery Heart* (an old New Orleans Scottish Rite honor investiture for 32nds or 33rds) would he create the KCCH (for 32nds) and Grand Cross (for 33rds). In addition, Albert Pike served as a Deputy of the Supreme Council when he was a 32nd. Today, a Deputy of the Supreme Council has almost always received the 33°.

As to where the 1857 Session was held; the location is 333 St Charles Ave, or the former home of the Grand Lodge of Louisiana. While the location is the same, the building is not. The present building was constructed in 1921. The old Masonic Temple Building was torn down for the new one. But, why there? The Grand Consistory met in the hall of Etoile Polaire Lodge #1 (and did so until its move to 619 Carondelet Street). They chose not to meet at Etoile Polaire. Prior to the Concordat of 1855, the Supreme Council of Louisiana met in the hall of Perseverance Lodge #4. Maybe they felt it inappropriate to meet there (it should be noted that even when the Supreme Council of Louisiana 33rds who did *not* participate in the Concordat announced that the Supreme Council of Louisiana had never ceased to exist and began openly holding meetings, they also did not meet again at Perseverance Lodge).Maybe holding the 1857 Session at the Grand Lodge building was an attempt to bring everyone together (something that didn't happen).

The election of Albert Pike as a 33rd was also something of a new practice for the Southern Jurisdiction. Just a short time before Pike received the degree, the Southern Jurisdiction made a change in how they would advance someone to the 33°. It was the beginning of what would today be known as "White Caps." Prior to this time, when one received the 33°, he would also become an Active Member of the Supreme Council. The 33rd degree and the office of Sovereign Grand Inspector General were received at the same time. With the change in practice, one would receive the 33rd degree, but not the office of SGIG (Active Member of the Supreme Council). He would become an Honorary Member of the Supreme Council or Honorary Sovereign Grand Inspector General. It is sometimes written that Albert Pike made this change in practice. That is incorrect. While Pike did make many changes, this was not one of them. He was one of the first to receive the 33°, but not the office of Sovereign Grand Inspector General. Pike would, however, be elected an Active Member (Sovereign Grand Inspector General) of the Southern Jurisdiction on March 20, 1858 and on January 2, 1859 he would be the first one *elected* as Sovereign Grand Commander of the Southern Jurisdiction (prior to that time, the Lt. Grand Commander automatically assumed the office of Grand Commander as per Article III of the *Grand Constitutions of 1786.*).

The past can either be just yesterday or an incredible story in need of telling. The history of the Scottish Rite in Louisiana is such an incredible story. The complete details of our amazing development and unique practices are, for a great part, still a mystery to us. So much is just unknown. This small paper on the 1857 Supreme Council Session in New Orleans can not hope to do justice to the whole story of what we know as the Ancient and Accepted Scottish Rite in Louisiana. All of the why's, when's, how's and more are simply not fully understood. The most that can be hoped for is to whet your appetite to learn and research more as to why we are so very unique and important. It is a journey available to us all and the only thing that we need to do is take the first historical step.

ORDO AB CHAO.

AD UNIVERSI TERRARUM ORBIS SUMMI ARCHITECTI GLORIAM.

DEUS MEUMQUE JUS.

PROCEEDINGS

OF THE

ANNUAL SESSION

OF THE

SUPREME COUNCIL

OF

Sovereign Grand Inspectors General,

33d and Last Degree of the Ancient and Accepted Rite,

FOR THE SOUTHERN JURISDICTION OF THE U. S. A.

HELD AT THE VALLEY OF NEW ORLEANS,

On the 29th, 31st and 2d days of the month called "Sebat," A∴ M∴ 5617, corresponding to the 14th, 15th and 17th days of February, in the Vulgar Era, 1857.

NEW ORLEANS:
PRINTED AT THE BULLETIN BOOK AND JOB OFFICE.
1857.

PROCEEDINGS.

SATURDAY, 29th "Sebat," A∴ M∴, 5617.
February 14th, 1857, V∴ E∴.

The Supreme Council was this day convened at half-past six o'clock, P.M., pursuant to a Decree from Charleston, S. C., in the Grand Council Chamber, Grand Lodge Buildings, Corner of St. Charles and Perdido streets, City of New Orleans and State of Louisiana, the avenues being, as usual, duly guarded by a body of K∴ K-H∴.

WERE PRESENT:

The following Ill∴ BB∴.

ALBERT G. MACKEY, C. SAMORY,	Sov∴ G∴ Insp∴ Gen∴ 33rd D∴, and active Members of the Supreme Council, at Charleston.
CH. LAFFON DE LADEBAT, A. R. MOREL, J. L. TISSOT, P. M. CHASSANIOL. CHARLES CLAIBORNE,	Sov∴ G∴ Insp∴ Gen∴ 33rd D∴, and Honorary Members and Deputies of the aforesaid Supreme Council for the State of Louisiana.
A. COSTA, P. D. FORMEL, A. P. LANAUX, G. COLLIGNON,	Sov∴ G∴ Insp∴ Gen∴ 33rd D∴, and Honorary members of the aforesaid Supreme Council.

The Supreme Council was opened in ample form by Ill∴ Bro∴ Albert G. Mackey, 33rd, acting as M∴ P∴ S∴ G∴ C∴ by special authority of a Decree, dated Charleston, 20th Hesvan, A∴ M∴, 5617; after which, Ill∴ Bro∴ C. Samory, 33rd, took the Chair as M∴ P∴ S∴ G∴ C∴, *pro tem.*

The M∴ P∴ S∴ G∴ C∴ then informed the Ill∴ BB∴ present, that by virtue of the authority vested in the Deputies of this Supreme Council for the State of Louisiana, they held a meeting on the 7th " Sebat," instant, and selected the following K∴ K-H∴ and Sub∴ P∴ of the R∴ S∴, viz.,

ALBERT PIKE	32d	T. F. BRAGG	32d
HARMON DOANE	"	C. WOLTERS	"
J. Q. A. FELLOWS	"	J. B. ROBERTSON	"
J. C. BATCHELOR	"	A. SCHREIBER	"
EDWARD BARNETT	"	L. LAY	"
L. H. PLACE	"	R. F. McGUIRE	"
C. B. CLAPP	"	F. H. KNAPP	"
WM. M. PERKINS	"	J. T. MONROE	"

to be initiated into the 33d and last Degree of the A∴ and A∴ Rite.

And the M∴ P∴ S∴ G∴ C∴ further observed that he was happy to state that, at the aforesaid meeting of the Deputies of this Supreme Council, it was unanimously resolved that, considering the services rendered to the cause of the A∴ and A∴ Rite, in this State, by Ill∴ Bro∴ Edw. Barnett, 32d, at the time of the Union of the two Consistories then existing, the 33rd D∴ be conferred on him as a special token of regard and esteem.

The M∴ P∴ S∴ G∴ C∴ then informed the Supreme Council that, should no objection be made, the above named Ill∴ BB∴ would, at once, be exalted to the 33rd and last D∴ of the A∴ and A∴ Rite.

No objection having been made, said K∴ K-H∴ and Sub∴ P∴ of the R∴ S∴.

HARMON DOANE	32d	T. F. BRAGG	32d
J. Q. A. FELLOWS	"	C. WOLTERS	"
J. C. BATCHELOR	"	J. B. ROBERTSON	"
L. H. PLACE	"	L. LAY	"
C. B. CLAPP	"	F. H. KNAPP	"
WM. M. PERKINS	"		

were duly initiated into the 33rd and last D∴ of the A∴ and A∴ Rite, constituted and proclaimed Sovereign Grand Inspectors General and Honorary Members of this Supreme Council.

Ill∴ BB∴ Albert Pike, Edward Barnett, A. Schreiber, R. F. McGuire, John T. Monroe, having been unavoidably prevented from attending, it was unanimously resolved that they should be initiated on Tuesday next, February 17, 1857, V∴ E∴

The Deputies of this Supreme Council having suggested the necessity of holding a General Grand Communication for the purpose of addressing Brethren of all Rites and Degrees of Masonry on matters of the greatest importance to the welfare of the Order in this Jurisdiction, it was unanimously—

Resolved, That a General Grand Communication of this Supreme Council be holden the next day, 15th February, 1857, V∴ E∴, at ten o'clock, A. M., at the Grand Lodge Hall, and that the Brethren of all Rites and Degrees of Masonry be fraternally invited to attend.

Resolved, That Ill∴ Bro∴ C. Samory, 33rd, be respectfully requested to deliver an Address in the French Language, to the General Grand Communication, and that Ill∴ Bro∴ Albert G. Mackey, 33rd, be invited to deliver to the same a translation of said Address in the English language.

To which these Ill∴ BB∴ kindly consented.

Ill∴ B∴ Laffon de Ladébat, 33rd, on leave being granted, informed the M∴ P∴ S∴ G∴ C∴ and the Members of this Supreme Council, that he had received a balustre from Ill∴ Bro∴ Albert Pike, 32d, one of the members elect to receive the 33rd D∴, and now at Washington, whereby it appeared that he would be unable to be in New Orleans before the month of March next, and said Ill∴ Bro∴ Laffon de Ladébat

6   PROCEEDINGS OF THE SUPREME COUNCIL

moved that the Deputies of this Supreme Council be authorized to confer the 33rd and last D.∴ on said Ill. Bro.∴ Albert
Pike, on his return to this City.

Ill.∴ Bro.∴ L. also moved that the Deputies of this Supreme Council be authorized to fill the vacancies among
themselves, by appointing new members of the 33rd and
last D.∴, the appointment, in all cases, to be approved by
the Supreme Council, at Charleston.

Both motions were duly seconded and unanimously
adopted.

The Supreme Council then adjourned till the next day,
at 10 o'clock A. M., and the Members retired in peace, glorifying the name of God.

CH. LAFFON DE LADEBAT, 33RD,

Sec.∴ G.∴ H.∴ E.∴, pro tem.

Sunday, 21st "Sebat," A∴ M∴, 5617.
February 15th, 1857, V∴ E∴

The Supreme Council was opened in ample form, by Ill∴
Bro∴ C. Samory, 33rd, acting as M∴ P∴ S∴ G∴ C∴.

WERE PRESENT:

ILL∴ BB∴ ALBERT G. MACKEY..............33d
"   "   C. SAMORY.................."
"   "   A. R. MOREL.................."
"   "   C. LAFFON DE LADEBAT............"
"   "   J. L. TISSOT.................."
"   "   P. M. CHASSANIOL............"
"   "   A. COSTA.................."
"   "   R. PREAUX.................."
"   "   P. D. FORMEL.................."
"   "   M. PRADOS.................."
"   "   H. DOANE.................."
"   "   J. Q. A. FELLOWS............"
"   "   THOMAS F. BRAGG............"
"   "   J. C. BATCHELOR............"
"   "   C. B. CLAPP.................."
"   "   F. H. KNAPP.................."

The minutes of the last session were read and approved.
The consideration of business was postponed until after
the General Grand Communication.

Whereupon, the M∴ P∴ S∴ G∴ C∴ ordered the Supreme
Council to move in procession, duly escorted by a body of
K∴ K-H∴ to the Hall of the M∴ W∴ Grand Lodge of
Louisiana, for the purpose of holding the General Grand
Communication.

GENERAL GRAND COMMUNICATION.

———

Ill∴ Bro∴ Albert G. Mackey, 33rd, acting as M∴ P∴ S∴ G∴ C∴ opened the Supreme Council in the first Degree of Masonry.

After which, the M∴ P∴ S∴ G∴ C∴ informed the meeting that, at a special session of this Supreme Council, holden at Charleston, on Tuesday, 20th Hesvan, A∴ M∴, 5617, November 18th, 1856, V∴ E∴, Ill∴ Bro∴ C. Samory, 33rd, was unanimously elected an active Member of the Supreme Council for the Southern Jurisdiction of the U. S. A., to supply a vacancy occasioned by the death of late Ill∴ Bro∴ J. C. Norris.

After some appropriate remarks on this happy selection, which were warmly responded to by Ill∴ Bro∴ C. Samory, 33rd, the M∴ P∴ S∴ G∴ C∴ proclaimed said Ill∴ Bro∴ in due form, and commanded the members and bodies under this jurisdiction, to acknowledge and obey said Ill∴ Bro∴ in his aforesaid capacity.

The M∴ P∴ S∴ G∴ C∴ then informed the Members of the General Grand Communication of the object of the meeting, and requested their kind attention to the Address to be delivered by Ill∴ Bro∴ C. Samory, 33rd.

This Ill∴ Bro∴ then took the floor and delivered, in the French language, an Address, of which the following is a correct translation, as given on the spot, by Ill∴ Bro∴ Albert G. Mackey, 33rd.

ADDRESS.

MY BRETHREN OF ALL RITES AND DEGREES:

Under ordinary circumstances, the Supreme Council of the 33rd and last Degree of the Ancient and Accepted Rite, for this jurisdiction, would have been content to have called a meeting of such Brethren as were exclusively under its immediate jurisdiction; but present circumstances require that we should make an appeal to all Masons, irrespective of Rites, and should point out those dangers which seem to threaten the Order. In pursuance of this duty, we now declare, that such dangers exist, and call upon you as Masons devoted to our sacred cause, to take these dangers into serious consideration and to apply the proper remedy.

Whatever the Rite may be to which we belong, whatever may be the jurisdiction which we obey, we must at all hazards maintain peace and harmony among ourselves. One of the fruits of the peace which has existed in this jurisdiction since the Concordat of February, 1856, V. E., has been the initiation of a large number of Brethren of other Rites into the sublime teachings of Scotch Masonry.

Many of our Brethren, misled we know not by what fatal influence, would again create a new schism and encroach upon the prerogatives of the M∴ W∴ Grand Lodge of this State, and in like manner upon those of our Supreme Council. Hence you perceive the nature of our danger, and understand somewhat of the object of this Grand Communication.

Our desire is to let the truth be known at once by those who are in doubt, and to place our Supreme Council and the Grand Lodge of this State in an impregnable position, that those who may conspire to interrupt the harmony which now prevails, may be compelled to refrain from pursuing their evil design, and may return to the path of duty. You will perceive that those who assail our Supreme Council, by the very same act attack the Grand Lodge of this State. It is indeed a happy coincidence that the interest of these two Sovereign Bodies is identically the same, and that the adherents to each are thus bound to act in unison when peace and harmony are to be maintained.

2

10   PROCEEDINGS OF THE SUPREME COUNCIL.

From the year 1839, V∴ E∴, till February, 1855, V∴ E∴, there existed in Louisiana, a Supreme Council, which had arrogated to itself rights exclusively belonging to the Grand Lodge. This Supreme Council not only pretended to administer the higher degrees of the Ancient and Accepted Rite, but also the three Symbolic Degrees. The Concordat which took place in February, 1855, V∴ E∴, between that Supreme Council and our own, put an end to that state of things, and since then the M∴ W∴ G∴ Lodge of Louisiana has, without opposition, exclusively held all the Symbolic Lodges under its jurisdiction, and the Supreme Council retained its authority over the higher bodies of the Ancient and Accepted Rite.

We now understand, however, that a new schism is about to break forth, and that trampling under foot the most sacred obligations, certain disturbers of public tranquillity contemplate proclaiming and acknowledging the authority of the so-called Supreme Council of New Orleans, and design thereby to repudiate not only the jurisdiction of our Supreme Council, but that of the M∴ W∴ Grand Lodge of the State. That Supreme Council, which has no authority, and which is not recognized by any of the existing Supreme Councils, claims jurisdiction over the first three Symbolic Degrees, as well as over the higher Degrees of the Ancient and Accepted Rite.

A few weeks ago the so-called Supreme Council constituted in this valley a spurious Chapter of Rose-croix, under the name and title of St. Andrew Chapter of Rose-croix, No. 5, and at this very moment that Supreme Council constitutes a Symbolic Lodge, "Le Foyer Maçonnique," which, no later than yesterday, was under the jurisdiction of M∴ W∴ G∴ Lodge. Let us hope, however, that the members of that Lodge will soon discover that they are strangely deceived.

Let us here warn those who receive Degrees in Masonic bodies not recognized by the M∴ W∴ Grand Lodge of this State, and by our Supreme Council, that they shall not be recognized by, nor admitted as visitors in, any of the bodies of the Ancient and Accepted Rite in both Hemispheres, as said bodies have no authority whatsoever to confer any of the Degrees of our Rite, and as they will be denounced throughout the World by the Grand Consistory of Louisiana, and by our Supreme Council.

And here we may state a very curious exemplification of the reckless and restless spirit of those disturbers of the public tranquillity. In 1850 and 1851, V∴ E∴, they seceded from the Grand Lodge and joined the so-called Supreme Council; in 1853 and 1854, they seceded from the so-called Supreme Council, and joined the Grand Lodge again, and now it seems they are about to recede once more from the Grand Lodge to join again the so-called Supreme Council. This battle-door and shuttle-cock game is most assuredly unworthy of intelligent Masons. But we know not which is the greater subject of wonder, those who can thus deceive, or those who allow themselves to be used as tools for the gratification of the vanities and whims of the deceivers.

The object of those deceivers is plain; they wish to substitute error for truth, wrong for right; they wish to avail themselves of the ignorance of some Brethren, and of the indifference of others, who are always ready to act without examination.

We, therefore, can hesitate no longer; the interest, as well as the welfare and prosperity of the Masonic Order, make it a law for us to enforce the rights of the M.·. W.·. Grand Lodge of this State over the three Symbolic Degrees, and to demonstrate that the authority of our Supreme Council to administer the higher Degrees of the Ancient and Accepted Rite of Masonry from the 4th to the 33rd Degree, inclusively, rests on an impregnable basis. If we prove, on the one hand, that there can be but one Supreme Council for the Southern Jurisdiction of the United States, and that one sitting now in Charleston, S. C.; and if, on the other hand, whatever our rights may be, we disclaim and waive all authority over the first three Symbolic Degrees, we trust no one having the due exercise of reason will repudiate the authority either of the Grand Lodge or of our Supreme Council, thus defined.

For that purpose, we propose to give a sketch of the Ancient and Accepted Rite, and to lay before you the Masonic events which took place in Louisiana since 1839, V.·. E.·. We have, therefore, obtained authentic documents, which, we have no doubt, will clearly convince all who act in good faith of the truth of what we assert, that we are in the right, and that the present organization of Masonry, in Louisiana, is the only means of securing peace and harmony among us. We may thus restrain those who are tempted to listen to the fraudulent assertions of these disturbers of Masonic peace, and we boldly challenge them to controvert the facts we are about to lay before you.

The Scotch Rite, or Rite of Perfection, also called the Ancient and Accepted Rite, was brought to America, in 1761, by a French Jew, Bro.·. Stephen Morin, in accordance with the powers with which he had been

---

invested by the Grand Consistory of Sublime Princes of the Royal Secret, convened at Paris under the Presidency of Chaillou de Joinville, Substitute General of the Order. The Scotch Rite was then composed of twenty-five Degrees only, the last of which was that of Sublime Prince of the R∴ S∴

When Morin arrived at St. Domingo, agreeably to his patent and according to his instructions, he appointed Brother M. M. Hayes, as a Deputy Inspector General, for North America, with the power of appointing others, wherever necessary. Brother Morin also appointed Brother Frankin as a Deputy Inspector General for Jamaica and the British Islands, and Brother Col. Provost for the Windward Islands and the British Army.

On the 25th October, 1762, V∴ E∴, the Grand Masonic Constitutions were finally ratified in Bordeaux, and proclaimed for the government of all the Lodges of Sublime and Perfect Masons, Councils, Colleges and Consistories of Sublime Princes of the Royal Secret, over the two Hemispheres. This was done with the consent and approval of the G∴ Consistory at Berlin. These Constitutions were transmitted, the same year, to Stephen Morin, who furnished with an authentic copy of the same all the Deputy-Inspectors appointed by him and by his Deputies. These Constitutions, of which we possess an authentic copy, duly signed by Isaac Long, one of Morin's Deputies, are still in force, as far as they are not modified or repealed by those of 1786.

Brother Hayes appointed Brother Da Costa, Deputy Inspector General for South Carolina, who, in 1788, and in accordance with the Constitutions of 1762, established a Sublime Grand Lodge of Perfection in Charleston. This body was the first of the Rite that was constituted in the United States.

After the death of Brother Da Costa, Brother Joseph Myers was appointed to succeed him by Brother Hayes, who also appointed Brother Solomon Bush, Deputy Inspector General for Pennsylvania, and Brother Berend M. Spitzer, for Georgia, which appointments were confirmed by a Council of Inspectors General that convened at Philadelphia, on the 15th of June, 1781, V∴ E∴ On the second of August, 1795, V∴ E∴, Ill∴ Bro∴, John Mitchell, was appointed Deputy Inspector General, for the State of South Carolina, vice Ill∴ Brother Berend M. Spitzer. These facts are incontrovertible, and are substantiated by all Masonic writers, and the researches which have been made in the Annals of the Order, go to prove, that notwithstanding the appointment of Inspectors General for the several

States, the Scotch Rite was worked in Charleston only. In that City only was established, in the year 1783, V∴E∴, a Sublime Grand Lodge of Perfection, wherein, for the first time in America, were conferred the Degrees of our Rite above the first three Symbolic Degrees. On the 20th of February, 1788, V∴E∴, a Council of Princes of Jerusalem was duly installed, also in Charleston, by Ill∴BB∴ J. Myers, Berned M. Spitzer, and A. Frost. To the zeal, therefore, of our Brethren of Charleston, to their constant application to the Scotch Rite, are we indebted for the foundation of the first Body of our Rite in America. This Body is, therefore, the basis, the parent of all Bodies of the Scotch Rite now in existence.

And now, my Brethren, that we have stated the introduction of the Scotch Rite, the foundation of the first Body of the Rite in the United States, let us go back to the year 1786, when the Grand Constitutions of the 33rd Degree were ratified and promulgated.

Trusting to the opinions of certain authors hostile to our Rite, some have attempted, and still attempt, to show that the Constitutions of 1786 are not the proper act of Frederick the Second, and of those Illustrious Brothers who composed the first Supreme Council, opened in Berlin ; that this instrument is a forgery and deserves no credit, and that, consequently, it cannot be regarded as the supreme organic law of our Rite.

The Brother who has proclaimed and still proclaims this doctrine, and who continues to do all in his power to inculcate it, has not always entertained this opinion. He is the author of a Decree, dated Dec. 3rd, 1851, the 10th Article of which reads as follows: "The Free, Ancient and Accepted Scotch Rite is now founded upon the Constitutions of 1762, the new Institutes of Frederick, in the year 1776, the Grand Constitutions, approved the same year by the said Frederick, and the Treaty of Alliance and Confederation, signed on the 22nd day of February, 1833, of the Christian Era."* It is true that, at that time, these Constitutions not being in his way, he had no scruples in admitting their validity. But two years after, in 1853, having other purposes to accomplish, he apparently changed his mind, and without any previous deliberation, and without asking the authorisation of the late Supreme Council of New Orleans, he altered and modified the text of the Article just quoted, in the French

---

* By referring to the original document in our hands, it will be seen that it is not in the year 1833, but in the year 1834, that this Treaty was signed. This error is insignificant, and we will rectify it hereafter in this Address.

translation which he made of that Article. This new version, as it appears in the French translation, reads as follows: "The Ancient and Accepted Scotch Rite is principally founded upon the Constitutions of 1762, and on the usages and Decrees of the Grand Orient of France, in all that relates to the nomenclature."

The late Supreme Council of New Orleans, which had adopted and sanctioned the Decree of 1851, admitting the Constitutions of 1786, never authorized the alteration made in 1853 in that Decree. The body, and all its members, were strangers to this change made in its solemn declaration of 1851, and which was never cancelled; and hence, it necessarily follows, that the Supreme Council of New Orleans, up to the time of its dissolution, constantly recognized the Constitutions of 1786; and it was only with a view to act in accordance with them, that the late Supreme Council transferred its powers to our Supreme Council, in order that both bodies should form but one: therefore, when you are told that the Supreme Council of New Orleans did not admit the validity of the Constitutions of 1786, you can safely deny the statement, by referring to the English text of the Decree of 1851, printed by Brother J. Lamarro, in that year, and to the 3rd paragraph of page 4, for a corroboration of your denial.

The Constitutions of Frederick are authentic and genuine, and the evidence we are about to offer must satisfy you and completely disprove the assertions of those who maintain the contrary. The evidence of their authenticity is to be found in the Treaty of Masonic Union, Alliance and Confederation, made in Paris on the 23rd of February, 1834, signed by Illustrious Brothers Fréteau de Pény, Count Ste. Rose de St. Laurent, General Lafayette, Charles N. Jubé, Philip Dupin, Dupin the Elder, Duke de Choiseul-Stainville, and others, who assert that these Constitutions are real and genuine, and after having compared the copy, which was annexed to the above named Treaty, with the original in the hands of Illustrious Brother Count de St. Laurent.

No one can doubt the testimony of these witnesses, whose names we have just given, nor can any faith after this be placed in the words or opinions of those who hesitate not to alter authentic documents whenever their purposes require it. To doubt the genuineness of the Constitutions of 1786, is, therefore, impossible, and equally impossible is it to prove that they are fraudulent or forged, as has been asserted, and if the least doubt is entertained by any of our Brethren, we have an authentic copy of the Treaty of 1834, and thus the truth of our assertion can be easily established.

The Grand Constitutions were ratified and signed at Berlin, on the first of May, 1786, by Frederick II, King of Prussia, who, as Grand Commander of the Order of Princes of the Royal Secret, was the Supreme Chief of the Scotch Rite. By these Constitutions, Frederick resigned his authority, and his Masonic prerogatives were deposited with a Council in and for each nation, consisting of nine Brethren. By these Constitutions, also, the number of our Degrees, which, heretofore, consisted of 25 only, was extended to 33,—the last of which is that of Sov∴ G∴ Inspector General.

It is, therefore, self-evident that the Dignity of Sov∴ G∴ Inspector General of 33rd Degree was created, and the formation of Supreme Councils authorized, by the Constitutions of 1786. It is also certain that no Sov∴ G∴ Inspectors General of the 33rd Degree, nor any Supreme Council, can exist, except by the authority of those Constitutions.

Now, if our opponents deny those very Constitutions, how can they claim the right of being Sov∴ G∴ Inspectors General of the 33rd D∴ and of forming Supreme Councils?

This, we believe, is a question which they will most assuredly find very difficult to solve.

The first Supreme Council, now existing, which was formed agreeably to the Constitutions of 1786, is our own, and was founded at Charleston, on the 31st of May, 1801, by BB∴ John Mitchell and Frederick Dalcho, the former a Colonel in the American Army, and the latter a Protestant Clergyman and most distinguished writer.

As a proof of the priority of our Supreme Council, we have the testimony of the best Masonic authors, and for proof of what we assert, we hold at the disposition of our BB∴ all the documents we possess on the subject.

It is then a positive fact which every one must admit, even among our opponents, that the first Supreme Council which appeared in the Masonic World is our Supreme Council. It is, consequently, the parent of all the other Supreme Councils which were established after its foundation; all spring from it. Its priority, legality and authority are, consequently, beyond all doubt.

But in order to prove that this conclusion is correct, we may state further, that BB∴ de Grasse-Tilly, Hacquet, and de la Hogue, received the 33d Degree from our Supreme Council in 1802, and that those BB∴ established the Supreme Council of France, and those of the French and

English Colonies. The Supreme Council of France was duly installed by Ill∴ Bro∴ de Grasse-Tilly, on the 22d of December, 1804, V∴ E∴, at Paris, in the Hall known as the Gallery of Pompeii, situated in the Rue-Neuve des Petits Champs, by virtue of Letters Patent to that effect from our Supreme Council, dated February 21st, 1802, V∴ E∴. This Supreme Council was the first and only one established in France, and it was afterwards divided into two branches, one called the Supreme Council of France, and the other the Supreme Council of the Grand Orient of France. These two bodies are still in existence. Ill∴ Bro∴ de-Grasse also established the Supreme Councils of Italy, Naples, Spain, and the Netherlands.

Thus the two Supreme Councils of France, as well as all the other Supreme Councils of the world, derive their being, either directly or indirectly, from our Supreme Council, and no Brother possessed of the 33d Degree can repudiate or overlook the authority by virtue of which he has been invested with his dignity, without, at the same time, resigning said dignity and all his prerogatives.

Article V of the Constitutions of 1786 provides that there shall be only one Supreme Council of the 33d Degree in each Nation or Kingdom; two in the United States of America, as distant as possible one from the other; one in the British Islands of America, and one also in the French Colonies.

As already stated, the first Supreme Council which was created by virtue of these Constitutions, is our own. It began its labors on the 31st of May, 1801, and its jurisdiction extended over the whole of the United States of America, until the 5th of August, 1813, when it established and constituted a Supreme Council in the City of New York, through its special proxy and representative, Emmanuel de la Motta. This Supreme Council, whose M∴ P∴ S∴ G∴ Commander was Ill∴ Brother D. D. Tompkins, Vice President of the United States of America, replaced the Grand Consistory of Sub∴ P∴ of the R∴ S∴, 32d Degree, which had been established in that city by our Supreme Council, on 6th of August, 1806, V∴ E∴. The seat of this Supreme Council has been lately removed to Boston; its jurisdiction is distributed over the Northern part of the United States of America, whilst that of Charleston is now confined to the Southern part of this country. The Supreme Council for the Northern Jurisdiction of the United States of America, created the Supreme Council of England and Wales; and this Body, in its turn, created the Supreme Council of Scotland and Ireland, with both which Bodies we are in correspondence.

The labors of the two Supreme Councils of the U. S. A. have never been interrupted, and, from the first day of their creation, up to this time, both have enjoyed the rights and privileges belonging to Supreme Councils, as the constituent and administrative heads of the Ancient and Accepted Rite, each in its respective jurisdiction; and whenever an attempt has been made to invalidate their authority and prerogatives, it has been met with a denunciation of the individuals or bodies encroaching upon their rights.

For instance, on the 21st of September, 1813, V∴ E∴, they denounced Cerneau, who had the pretension to establish a Supreme Council at New York, and the consequence of this denunciation was to unmask an impostor, trading in Masonry.

The denunciation of Cerneau by our Supreme Council, was approved and sanctioned by a Decree of the Supreme Council of France, dated December 24th, 1813, V∴ E∴, and this Decree shows that a third Supreme Council of the 33rd Degree cannot exist in the United States of America.*

The Supreme Council of Cerneau had but a short existence, but his numerous victims have not forgotten his impostures, even at this day.

In 1827, another attempt to revive the Supreme Council of Cerneau was made by Henry C. Atwood; this did not succeed. However, this usurpation of the rights of the Supreme Council for the Northern jurisdiction of the United States of America was immediately denounced in a protest, under date of August 6th, 1827, and signed by J. J. J. Gourgas, M∴ P∴ S∴ G∴ Commander.

The Supreme Council of Atwood, which appointed J. Cresso to succeed him, was unable to resist this denunciation, and ceased its labors.

Another Supreme Council sprung up also in New York, under the presidency of Elias Hicks; it had but a nominal existence. It was, likewise, denounced as having no legal authority.

When the Supreme Council of New Orleans brought itself into notice through its antagonism to the Grand Lodge of the State of Louisiana,

---

* See in the proceedings of the Supreme Council of France, the very interesting trial of the M∴ P∴ S∴ G∴ Commander, Count de Grasse-Tilly. We propose to publish this trial in the English and French languages for the information of all concerned.

3

its illegality and spuriousness were also denounced to the Masonic world
by the circulars issued on the 18th and 26th April, 1851, by the Supreme
Councils for the Southern and Northern jurisdictions of the United States
of America.

Since, therefore, the 5th of August, 1813, the provisions of Article V.
of the Constitutions of 1786 have been complied with; and there are in
the United States of America, consequently, but two Supreme Councils.
They have ever preserved and enforced their authority, and they have
never failed to discountenance all attempts against an authority which belongs to them.

It was impossible for a third Supreme Council to be established in the
United States of America without violating the Constitutions of 1786,
without which, as already stated, neither the 33rd Degree nor Supreme
Councils can exist. Nevertheless, on the 27th October, 1839, BB. O. de
Santangelo, R. Perdreauville, Roca Santi Petri, J. F. Canonge, F. Verrier,
A. Montmain, and others, established in New Orleans a Supreme Council,
which was pompously called "Supreme Council for the United States of
America."

In the act of foundation of this Supreme Council, the signers declare
that they form and constitute themselves into a Supreme Council of the
33rd Degree, by virtue of the Constitutions of 1786, which they proclaim
to be authentic and genuine; and they declare, besides, on behalf of this
Supreme Council, that they agree to the Treaty of Masonic Union,
Alliance and Confederation, made at Paris, on the 23rd of February, 1834.

It is evident that the Constitutions of 1786, by virtue of which the late
Supreme Council of New Orleans claimed to be established, prohibited,
instead of authorizing the creation of any such body, as the fifth Article
of the same provides that there shall be but two Supreme Councils in the
United States of America, and as in 1839 there had already existed one of
said bodies at Charleston, since 1801, and another at New York, since 1813.

Thus the late Supreme Council of New Orleans never had a legal existence, as it could not be created nor exist without violating the Constitutions
of 1786, which their founders had declared to be the supreme organic law
of the A. and A. Rite.

Those who established the late Supreme Council of New Orleans, acknowledged also the Treaty of Masonic Union, Alliance and Confederation
of 1834, and sanctioned the same, as above stated.

In order to become parties to said Treaty, and to clothe their Supreme

Council with the required legality, and thereby cause it to be recognized, they addressed, on the 26th of February, 1840, a baluster to the Supreme Council of France, notifying the latter body of their adhesion to said Treaty of Alliance of 1834, and demanding the recognition of their Supreme Council, and its admission to the Treaty.

We are in possession of the above-mentioned baluster, which has been returned to us by our BB∴ in France: it bears the names, all signed *manu propriâ*, of BB∴ De Santangelo, De Perdreauville, Santi Petri, Dubayle, Pichot, Montmain, Faget, and Canonge; and we have also been favored with the Decree of the Supreme Council of France, under date of July 25, 1845, and by which that Sovereign Body declines to recognize said Supreme Council, and to admit it in the Masonic Alliance of 1834; and further declares said Supreme Council to be spurious, clandestine, and illegal.

Thus the so-called Supreme Council for the United States of America, otherwise, the late Supreme Council of New Orleans, has never been recognized by the Supreme Council of France, nor by the Masonic bodies who were parties to the Treaty of 1834.

You have now the reason why an alteration was made in the text of paragraph 10 of the Decree of December 3d, 1851.

In 1851, the late Supreme Council of New Orleans declared "that the Free, Ancient and Accepted Scotch Rite was founded upon the Constitutions of 1762, the new Institutes of Frederick, in the year 1786, the Grand Constitutions given and approved in the same year by the said Frederick, and the Treaty of Alliance and Confederation signed on the 22d day of February, 1833, C∴ E∴"

This declaration, which, however, was similar to the one made in 1839, at the time of the formation of the late Supreme Council of New Orleans, and the refusal of the Supreme Council of France to recognize, and, consequently, to admit, said body as a party to the Treaty of 1834, gave the death blow to the Supreme Council of New Orleans. It was necessary to get out of this awkward position, the error of which was detected only in 1858, V∴ E∴, and it was for that purpose that the Decree of 1851, V∴ E∴, was altered.

Once provided with this Decree, thus altered, the members of the late Supreme Council of New Orleans believed themselves to be in a good and regular position; and, indeed, by means of this very alteration, they succeeded in procuring the recognition of their Supreme Council by that of the Grand Orient of France. But this Illustrious Body would never have granted their sanction, if they had known the truth, that is, the declaration of adhesion to the Treaty of 1834, as contained in the Decree of the late Supreme Council of New Orleans, under date December 3d, 1851, and for this reason : as already stated, there are two Supreme Councils in France, one in opposition to the other. The late Supreme Council of New Orleans first recognised one of them, as per their declaration of December 3d, 1851; and remember that this declaration has never been repealed; and it was only when their demand to be recognised was defeated, that, after clandestinely altering the text of their declaration, they applied to the other Supreme Council, which they, at first, had virtually declared to be the spurious Supreme Council.

All the foregoing shows plainly that there never existed any legal and lawful Supreme Council in New Orleans, and that there cannot exist any as long as the Constitutions of 1786 shall remain unchanged, or as long as the Supreme Councils of Boston and Charleston shall exist.

These considerations convinced the members of the late Supreme Council of New Orleans, of the illegality of their position, and prompted them to negotiate and to sign the Concordat of the 6th and 17th of February, 1855, V∴ E∴, the consequence of which was the dissolution of that body, and its merging into our Supreme Council.

By this Concordat, all the rights, privileges and prerogatives possessed or claimed by our BB∴ during the existence and under the authority of the late Supreme Council of New Orleans, were guaranteed to them, and we have the satisfaction to state that those of our BB∴ who wished to enjoy the rights stipulated in said Concordat, met with no obstacles whatever, and we may here assure those who have not yet fulfilled the required formalities, that they will be welcomed when they desire to do so.

Let us come now to the period when the late Supreme Council of New Orleans, whose existence was unknown, since it had never been recognised, as already stated, by any of the Supreme Councils with which it had sought an intercourse; let us, I say, come to that period when the late Supreme Council of New Orleans attempted to encroach upon the rights of the M∴ W∴ Grand Lodge of the State of Louisiana.

Up to that period, peace and harmony had prevailed among the Masons of this East: the Symbolic Lodges were working under the jurisdiction of the Grand Lodge of the State of Louisiana, whilst the late Supreme

Council of New Orleans administered all the Degrees of the Ancient and
Accepted Rite from the fourth up to the last. In June, 1850, V∴ E∴, a
Convention of Representatives of all the Symbolic Lodges of the State was
held at Baton Rouge, under the authority of the Grand Lodge of the State
of Louisiana. This Convention adopted a Constitution, wherein it was
declared, "That the Grand Lodge of Free and Accepted Masons for the
State of Louisiana recognized none other than Ancient Masonry, consisting
of three Symbolic Degrees only, and that it was forbidden to tolerate any
distinction derogatory to its character."

The late Supreme Council of New Orleans pretended that this declaration had been made witth a view to proscribe the Ancient and Accepted
Scotch Rite. But this was not correct, and we all know that the declaration of 1850 was intended to establish the fact that all Masons of the
three Degrees of all Rites were to unite together and to form but one and
the same family.

The Supreme Council of New Orleans made use of this frivolous pretext
to proclaim that, henceforth, it would constitute and administer the Symbolic Lodges of the Ancient and Accepted Rite, and that it would admit
to the Degrees above the third, only the members of the Lodges under its
jurisdiction, and called upon the Symbolic Lodges to recognize its
authority.

This usurpation of the rights of the Grand Lodge, together with the
contempt evinced for the solemn expression of the will of the Masons of
Louisiana, as stated in the Convention of 1850, caused general discontent,
created a schism and became a firebrand of discord among the Masons of
this jurisdiction.

Of the thirty Lodges which, at the time of the declaration, were working
under the jurisdiction of the Grand Lodge of the State of Louisiana, only
three repudiated the authority of the Grand Lodge and recognized the
jurisdiction of the Supreme Council.

These three Lodges were denounced and proclaimed to be spurious and
clandestine by the Grand Lodge of this State, and by the Grand Lodges
of the United States of America. All Masonic papers and publications
thundered against them.

The position of the BB∴ who composed these Lodges was indeed pain-
ful and unenviable; they were everywhere shut out; the Masonic Temples of the United States of America were closed against them; in one
word, they were denied admittance by all the Lodges of their own country.

The profanes who were initiated in these Lodges had a right to complain, and did complain when they discovered that, instead of acquiring the rights and privileges of Masons, their hopes were frustrated; and they declared unhesitatingly that they had been deceived.

Such was the mournful state of things after the strange proclamation of the Supreme Council, which never succeeded in procuring the approbation of the majority of the members of the Craft, and the proof is, that it never exercised jurisdiction over any other bodies than the three Lodges above named, and one of them afterwards abandoned the Supreme Council; whilst the number of Lodges under the jurisdiction of the Grand Lodge, which was only 30 at that time, increased to 70 in 1851, and is now 102.

This is the most conclusive proof that the attempts of the Supreme Council to exercise jurisdiction over the Symbolic Degrees, were discountenanced by an overwhelming majority.

All the efforts of this Supreme Council to enlist our American BB.·. were defeated. In 1850, this Supreme Council adopted the English language, although the great majority of the same were French, and did not understand that language.

But it was of vital importance to secure our American BB.·. Their influence was necessary. It appears, however, that a change has taken place; those who in 1850 had decided to use the English language exclusively, wish us now to use the French language alone, and blame us for speaking English to those who do not understand French.

On the 21st of September, 1853, Brother J. Foulhouze resigned his membership in the Supreme Council. On the 21st December, same year, BB.·. J. J. E. Massicot, Thomas Wharton Collens, and J. B. Faget resigned also. On the 7th of January, 1854, Bro.·. Stephen Herriman resigned. BB.·. Lisbony, Lamothe and others, were stricken off the Rolls on the 5th October, 1854, for non-payment of dues.

Consequently, the Supreme Council was composed of the following BB.·. only: C. Claiborne, C. Samory, C. Laffon de Ladébat, G. Collignon, A. Costa, L. E. Deluxain, P. D. Formel, John H. Holland, J. L. Tissot, A. P. Lanaux, John L. Lewis, F. A. Lamsden, C. Maurian, F. Meilleur, A. R. Morel, H. Peychaud, M. Prados, F. Ricau, P. M. Chassaniol, E. Preaux, E. Barthe, F. Garcia, Samuel Ward, and Joseph W. Walker. The four last named BB.·. were absent, at that time, and have not yet returned.

These BB.·., true to their duty, and sincerely devoted to the welfare of the Order, could not overlook the position of their BB∴ who, on account of their faithfulness to the late Supreme Council, were ostracized every where, and they resolved by all honorable means to restore them to the rights and privileges to which they were entitled.

For that purpose, these BB∴ of the late Supreme Council examined carefully :

1st. The act by which the late Supreme Council of New Orleans was established in 1839.

2d. The act by which its founders recognized the Constitutions of 1786 and the Treaty of Masonic Union, Alliance and Confederation of 1834.

3d. The Decree of this very Supreme Council under date of December 3d, 1851.

4th. The Decree by which, on the 20th July, 1845, the Supreme Council of France refused to recognize the late Supreme Council of New Orleans, and to admit it as a party to the Treaty of Masonic Union, Alliance and Confederation of 1834.

A Report was made and unanimously adopted, the consequence of which was a Resolution decreeing that the late Supreme Council had never had a legal existence, and that, in accordance with the ratification given by it, in 1839 and 1851, to the Constitutions of 1786, it could continue no longer to exercise a power which did not belong to it, without committing an act of usurpation, unless its authority were recognized and sanctioned by the Masonic authorities which contested its rights, and which alone could render its acts legal and lawful ; those Masonic authorities were the Supreme Councils for the Southern and Northern jurisdictions of the United States of America, and to obtain that sanction, a memorandum was addressed to those Sovereign Bodies, who, after mature consideration, decreed that a third Supreme Council could not exist in the United States of America, inasmuch as the 5th Article of the Constitutions of 1786 forbade it, and that, consequently, the petition of the Supreme Council of New Orleans could not be granted.

This refusal gave birth to the Concordat of 1855, by which the late Supreme Council of New Orleans transferred its powers and jurisdiction to that of Charleston, so that now those two bodies form but one body ; the bodies constituted by said late Supreme Council were recognized and maintained in all their rights and privileges, and all BB∴ having received degrees and dignities from said body, have been acknowledged as legally possessed of the same, after the necessary formalities.

This page is missing.

This page is missing.

In a Supplement of said book, entitled "The Ineffable Degrees," the author attempts to explain the Degrees of our Rite, from the 4th to the 33d, inclusively, the perusal of which, by any of our BB∴ regularly initiated in any of said Degrees, will convince them of Mr. J. L. Cross' total ignorance of our Rite,—of its ceremonies, and of its philosophy and object. He concludes with what he terms "A history of the Scotch Rite in America," in which he asserts that a Supreme Council was established at New Orleans in 1795, V∴ E∴, by the Grand Orient of France. This is a gross and palpable error. The first Supreme Council constituted by virtue of the Constitutions of 1786, V∴ E∴, was that of Charleston, which was opened 31st May, 1801, V∴ E∴; said Supreme Council conferred the 33d Degree on Count de Grasse-Tilly, and he was the founder of the first Supreme Council of France, which was formed on the 24th December, 1804, V∴ E∴.

There was no Supreme Council in France previous to said date, and therefore there existed no Masonic authority in that country to create a Supreme Council in New Orleans in 1795, V∴ E∴. Besides, there never existed any Supreme Council in New Orleans previous to the 27th of October, 1839, V∴ E∴, at which time a body of that Degree was established.

Mr. Cross further asserts that a quarrel occurred in 1807, V∴ E∴, between the Supreme Council of Louisiana and that of Charleston, that they appealed to the Grand Orient of France, which declined to interfere, and deputised Jos. Cerneau, the notorious Masonic impostor, to form a Supreme Council in the city of New York.

It is, indeed, difficult to conceive of such gross ignorance, or so bold an attempt to mislead. The published proceedings of the Grand Orient and Supreme Council of France, and numerous authentic documents, show that the denunciation of Jos. Cerneau, as an impostor, and of his Supreme Council, as a spurious and clandestine body, was approved and sanctioned by a Decree of the Grand Orient and Supreme Council of France, under date of 24th December, 1818, V∴ E∴, and that his Supreme Council was never recognized by any of the legal Masonic authorities in either hemisphere.

As to the allegation that an appeal was made in 1808, V∴ E∴, by the Supreme Councils of Charleston and New Orleans to the Grand Orient of France, it is the boldest attempt at deception which has ever been made. There could be no appeal made in 1808, V∴ E∴, by the Supreme Council of New Orleans to the Grand ſ

Orient of France, for the best of all reasons, to wit: that it was not until thirty-one years after that date that a Supreme Council was formed in said City. Authentic documents are in our possession to sustain the facts we assert, and to contradict the errors and misrepresentations of Mr Cross.

The object of these very incorrect statements of Mr. Jeremy L. Cross, was to announce that he was the Grand Commander for the Northern Jurisdiction of the United States of America, and to show, as he says, "that the existence of a regular Supreme Council in the city of New York is not a fable." Now, we not only assert, but we are prepared to prove, that the greater portion of Mr. Cross' history of the Scotch Rite, and the existence of a Supreme Council in New York, of which he is the Grand Commander, are "but fables," fabricated for the purpose of deceiving our Brethren.

The M∴ P∴ S∴ G∴ C∴ afterwards invited the Members present to take the floor, if they had any observations to offer for the interest of the Order.

Whereupon, Ill∴ Bro∴ S. P. Auchmuty, 32d, made some very appropriate remarks on the foregoing Address, which, he said, could not fail to throw full light on matters hitherto almost unknown to the majority of Masons in this Valley, and the consequence of which would be forever to remove not only all attempts at disturbance and even certain prejudices resulting only from ignorance, but above all, to draw closer the bonds of friendship between the Members of all Rites of Masonry. This Ill∴ Brother concluded in moving that said Address, together with all the necessary vouchers, be printed in the French and English languages and distributed among the fraternity.

Which motion was duly seconded and unanimously adopted, and the M∴ P∴ S∴ G∴ C∴ was respectfully requested to submit the same to the Supreme Council.

The General Grand Communication having no further business to act upon, the M∴ P∴ S∴ G∴ C∴ closed the

Supreme Council in the first degree of Masonry, and the
Sov.·. G.·. Inspectors General returned in procession, duly
escorted by a body of Knights Kadosh, to the Grand Council
Chamber.

On resuming the Chair, Ill.·. Brother Albert G. Mackey,
33d, offered the floor to any Members who might desire to
address the Supreme Council.

Whereupon, Ill.·. Brother C. Samory, 33d, offered the
following Preamble and Resolutions, which were unanimously adopted :

WHEREAS, The members of this Supreme Council consider the suggestion of Ill.·. Bro.·. Chas. W. Vigne, Sec.·. Gen.·. H.·. E.·. of the Supreme
Council for England and Wales, as contained in his letter of 21st January,
1856, V.·. E.·., to Ill.·. Brother Charles W. Moore, respecting a General
Grand Conference of all the existing Supreme Councils, as highly important and necessary for the welfare of the Order, and as the best means of
uniting said bodies into an alliance which would produce harmony and a
better understanding :

Resolved, That the suggestion of a General Grand Conference be respectfully submitted to the Supreme Council, at Charleston.

WHEREAS, By the Constitutions of 1786, all the rights, powers and
prerogatives of Frederick II, as Supreme Chief of the Ancient and Accepted Rite, are conferred on a Supreme Council of nine Brethren in each
nation, who possess, IN THEIR OWN DISTRICT, *all the Masonic prerogatives
that his Majesty individually possessed, and are* "SOVEREIGNS OF MA-
SONRY:"

WHEREAS, By said Constitutions, "*the Sovereigns of Masonry*," in the
United States of America, are the Supreme Councils for the Southern and
Northern Jurisdictions; and as such, have the right to make such amendments to said Constitutions as they may deem necessary for the better
administration of the Order in their jurisdiction :

WHEREAS, The spirit of our American institutions, the ideas, opinions,
customs, usages of the age, and the extension of our territory, require that
amendments should be made to the Constitutions of 1786, as far as regards
the administration of the Ancient and Accepted Rite in our own *district*
or *jurisdiction* :

Resolved, That the members of this Supreme Council respectfully suggest that a Conference be held between the Southern and Northern Councils, for the purpose of making such amendments to the Constitutions of 1786, as said bodies may deem necessary and proper.

WHEREAS, Information has been given to this Supreme Council of the existence in this Valley of a body styling itself St. Andrew Chapter of Rose-croix, No. 5, of which J. Lamarre is Secretary, and Jos. Lisbony is said to be the presiding officer :

WHEREAS, Said body, styling itself St. Andrew Chapter of Rose-croix, No. 5, is an illegal, spurious and clandestine body, having no legal authority to sit as a Chapter of Rose-croix, or to confer any of the Degrees of the Ancient and Accepted Rite :

WHEREAS, Said spurious and clandestine body, styling itself St. Andrew Chapter of Rose-croix, No. 5, has been denounced and proclaimed in both Hemispheres by this Supreme Council, in circulars addressed to all existing Masonic bodies :

Resolved, That all Brethren under the obedience of this Supreme Council, or of bodies under its jurisdiction, are forbidden to hold any Masonic intercourse relating to any Degrees of the Ancient and Accepted Rite above the third or Master's Degree, with the members of said body styling itself St. Andrew Chapter of Rose-croix, No. 5 ; to visit said body, or to admit any of its members as visitors in any of the bodies under the jurisdiction of this Supreme Council, under the penalties provided in the Statutes, Rules and Regulations of this Supreme Council.

Resolved, That all bodies under the jurisdiction of this Supreme Council are enjoined strictly to enforce the provisions of the preceding resolve.

On motion of Ill∴ Bro∴ Charles Laffon de Ladébat, duly seconded—

Resolved, That, in compliance with the unanimous vote of the General Grand Communication, the Address of Ill∴ Brother C. Samory, 33d, together with all the necessary vouchers, be printed in French and English, and distributed to the Fraternity.

The Supreme Council having no further business to act

upon, adjourned till Tuesday evening, 17th February, inst., and the Members retired in peace, glorifying the name of God.

CH. LAFFON DE LADEBAT, 33RD,

Sec∴ Gen∴ H∴ E∴, pro tem.

———————•—————

TUESDAY, 23rd "Sebat," A∴ M∴, 5617, }
February 17th, 1857, V∴ E∴.   }

The Supreme Council met pursuant to adjournment, and was opened in ample form, by Ill∴ Bro∴ Charles Laffon de Ladébat, 33rd, acting as M∴ P∴ S∴ G∴ C∴.

WERE PRESENT:

ILL∴ BB∴ ALBERT G. MACKEY.............................33d
  "   "   C. LAFFON DE LADEBAT .... "
  "   "   A. R. MOREL............................... "
  "   "   J. C. BATCHELOR........................... "
  "   "   C. B. CLAPP............................... "
  "   "   L. H. PLACE............................... "
  "   "   P. M. CHASSANIOL.......................... "
  "   "   H. DOANE.................................. "
  "   "   J. Q. A. FELLOWS.......................... "
  "   "   C. WOLTERS................................ "
  "   "   P. D. FORMEL.............................. "

The M∴ P∴ S∴ G∴ C∴ stated that the object of the meeting was to confer the 33d and last Degree on Sir Knights K-H∴ and Sub∴ P∴ of the R∴ S∴, Edward Barnett, A.

Schreiber, R. F. McGuire and John T. Monroe, who had been prevented from attending the ceremony of initiation on the Saturday previous, and invited the Ill∴ BB∴ to state their objections, if any they had, against the advancement of the aforesaid Ill∴ Brethren Candidates. No objection was made.

Ill∴ Brother A. R. Morel, Sec∴ Gen∴ H∴ E∴, *pro tem.*, begged leave to propose Sir Knight K-H∴ and Sub∴ P∴ Ezekiel Salomon, 32d, for initiation into the 33rd and last D∴, and he gave his reasons for making this proposition, which met with the unanimous approval of all present.

Ill∴ Bro∴ E. Salomon was, consequently, elected to receive the 33rd and last D∴ of the A∴ and A∴ Rite.

Whereupon, the M∴ P∴ S∴ G∴ C∴ proceeded, forthwith, with the initiation ceremonies, and the Members elect were duly constituted and proclaimed Sovereign Grand Inspectors General, 33rd D∴ of the A∴ and A∴ Rite, and Honorary Members of this Supreme Council.

And none of the Members present expressing a desire to address the meeting, and all the business on hand having been transacted, the M∴ P∴ S∴ G∴ C∴ adjourned the Supreme Council till the return of Ill∴ Bro∴ Albert Pike, 32d, and the Members retired in peace, glorifying the name of God.

A. R. MOREL, 33an,

Sec∴ Gen∴ H∴ E∴, pro tem.

•

SATURDAY, "Yiar" 1st, A∴ M∴ 5617, ⎫
April 25th, 1857, V∴ E∴ ⎬

The Supreme Council met pursuant to orders issued by
Ill∴ Bro∴ C. Samory, 33d, Active Member of the Supreme
Council for the Southern Jurisdiction of the U. S. A., sitting
at Charleston, S. C., at seven o'clock, P. M., in the Grand
Lodge Hall, corner of St. Charles and Perdido streets, City
of New Orleans, and State of Louisiana, the avenues being,
as usual, guarded by a detachment of Knights Kadosh.

WERE PRESENT:

ILL∴ BB∴ C. SAMORY...33d.
  "   "   CHARLES CLAIBORNE............................. "
  "   "   C. LAFFON DE LADEBAT...................... "
  "   "   A. R. MOREL.. "
  "   "   P. M. CHASSANIOL............................... "
  "   "   THOMAS F. BRAGG............................. "
  "   "   J. Q. A. FELLOWS............................... "
  "   "   JOHN H. HOLLAND............................... "
  "   "   H. DOANE... "
  "   "   C. B. CLAPP....................................... "
  "   "   C. WOLTERS....................................... "
  "   "   P. D. FORMEL...................................... "
  "   "   F. H. KNAPP....................................... "

The Supreme Council was opened in ample form by Ill∴
Bro∴ C. Samory, 33d, acting as M∴ P∴ S∴ G∴ Commander.

The M∴ P∴ S∴ G∴ Commander informed the Ill∴ BB∴ present that at a meeting of the Deputies of the Supreme Council at Charleston, held on the 14th February, 1857, V∴ E∴, authority had been given by Ill∴ Bro∴ Albert G. Mackey, 33d, Special Representative and Proxy of the aforesaid Supreme Council, to confer the 33d and last Degree of the A∴ and A∴ Rite on Sir Knight K-H∴ and Sub∴ P∴ Albert Pike.

The M∴ P∴ S∴ G∴ Commander further stated that the Deputies of the aforesaid Supreme Council had received a balustre from Sir Knight K-H∴ and Sub∴ P∴ Willis P. Coleman, showing that, in consequence of circumstances over which he had no control, he had been prevented from receiving the 33d Degree, to which he had been elected by said Deputies, on the 7th of February last, and that he had received from Ill∴ Bro∴ Albert G. Mackey, then in this Valley, the assurance that he would be initiated as soon as this Supreme Council would meet again for conferring the 33d Degree on Ill∴ Bro∴ Albert Pike, 32d.

The M∴ P∴ S∴ G∴ Commander also observed that the Deputies of this Supreme Council had acknowledged the rights of Ill∴ Bro∴ Willis P. Coleman, 32d.

Whereupon, the M∴ P∴ S∴ G∴ Commander informed the Members present, that if no objections were made, he would proceed at once with the ceremony of initiating Sir Knights and Sub∴ P∴ Albert Pike and Willis P. Coleman into the 33d and last Degree of the A∴ and A∴ Rite.

No opposition being made, Sir Knights and Sub∴ P∴ Albert Pike and Willis P. Coleman were duly initiated into the 33d and last Degree of the A∴ and A∴ Scotch Rite,

5

and proclaimed Sov∴ G∴ Inspectors General, and Honorary Members of the Supreme Council, at Charleston.

After which, Ill∴ Bro∴ C. Laffon de Ladébat, on leave being granted, proposed that the Deputies of this Supreme Council be invited to appoint a Deputy in the stead of Ill∴ Brother C. Samory, 33d, elected active Member of the Supreme Council, at Charleston—which was adopted.

Whereupon, Ill∴ Brother Harmon Doane was unanimously elected to fill the vacancy occasioned by the promotion of Ill∴ Brother C. Samory, 33d.

The M∴ P∴ S∴ G∴ Commander then read a balustre from Ill∴ Brother J. L. Tissot, 33d, tendering his resignation as Deputy of this Supreme Council, and respectfully suggesting that Ill∴ Brother J. Q. A. Fellows, 33d, be appointed in his stead. The resignation and request of Ill∴ Brother J. L. Tissot, 33d, were unanimously granted, and Ill∴ Brother J. Q. A. Fellows was appointed a Deputy of this Supreme Council.

The M∴ P∴ S∴ G∴ Commander read also a balustre from Ill∴ Brother Charles Laffon de Ladébat, 33d, tendering his resignation as Deputy of this Supreme Council for the purpose of enabling this Supreme Council to appoint Ill∴ Brother Albert Pike, whose election was better calculrted to promote the prosperity of the Order, in America. The motives of Ill∴ Bro∴ Laffon de Ladébat were duly appreciated by this Supreme Council; his resignation was, consequently, accepted, and Ill∴ Brother Albert Pike, 33d, appointed as Deputy of the Supreme Council, at Charleston, in his stead.

And none of the members present expressing a desire to

address the meeting, the M∴ P∴ S∴ G∴ Commander adjourned the Supreme Council *sine die*, and the Members retired in peace, glorifying the name of God.

CH. LAFFON DE LADEBAT, 33d,

Sec∴ Gen∴ H∴ E∴, pro tem.

A LIST OF THE MEMBERS

COMPOSING THE

Grand Consistory of Sub∴ P∴ of the R∴ S∴

32d Degree of the Ancient and Accepted Scotch Rite,

IN AND FOR THE STATE OF LOUISIANA,

All Sov∴ G∴ Insp∴ Gen∴ being Active Members "de Jure."

———————

FIRST CLASS,

C. SAMORY, 33d, Active Member of the Supreme Council at Charleston.

SECOND CLASS.

P. M. CHASSANIOL, 33d,	Hon∴ Member and Dep∴ of the Sup∴ C∴ at Charleston.						
CHAS. CLAIBORNE, 33d,	"	"	"	"	"	"	"
HARMON DOANE, 33d,	"	" *	"	"	"	"	"
J. Q. A. FELLOWS, 33d,	"	"	"	"	"	"	"
JOHN L. LEWIS, 33d,	"	"	"	"	"	"	"
F. A. LUMSDEN, 33d,	"	"	"	"	"	"	"
CHARLES MAURIAN, 33d,	"	"	"	"	"	"	"
A. B. MOREL, 33d,	"	"	"	"	"	"	"
ALBERT PIKE, 33d.	"	"	"	"	"	"	"

MEMBERS OF THE GRAND CONSISTORY OF LOUISIANA. 37

THIRD CLASS.

EDW. BARNETT, 33d, Hon∴ Member of the Sup∴ C∴ at Charleston.

J. C. BATCHELOR, 33d,

J. BEUGNOT, 33d,

THOS. F. BRAGG, 33d,

C. B. CLAPP, 33d,

W. P. COLEMAN, 33d,

G. COLLIGNON, 33d,

A. COSTA, 33d,

L. E. DELUZAIN, 33d,

P. D. FORMEL, 33d,

JOHN H. HOLLAND, 33d,

F. H. KNAPP, 33d,

C. LAFFON DE LADEBAT, 33d,

A. P. LANAUX, 33d,

L. LAY, 33d,

R. F. McGUIRE, 33d,

F. MEILLEUR, 33d,

JOHN T. MONROE, 33d,

W. M. PERKINS, 33d,

H. PEYCHAUD, 33d,

L. H. PLACE, 33d,

M. PRADOS, 33d,

R. PREAUX, 33d,

F. RICAU, 33d,

JOHN B. ROBERTSON, 33d,

E. SALOMON, 33d,

A. SCHREIBER, 33d,

J. L. TISSOT, 33d,

S. WARD, 33d,

C. WOLTERS, 33d.

FOURTH CLASS.

S. P. AUCHMUTY, 32d,	Active	Member.
J. S. BEERS, Jr., 32d,	"	"
JOS. CHELLET, 32d,	"	"
C. DE CHOISEUL, 32d,	"	"
P. DEVERGES, 32d,	"	"
A. F. ELLIOT, 32d,	"	"
J. A. FERGUSON, 32d,	"	"
JOHN GALPIN, 32d,	"	"
JUAN GOMILA, 32d,	"	"
F. LEVASSEUR, 32d,	"	"
H. T. LONSDALE, 32d,	"	"
F. L. K. LUDWIGSEN, 32d,	"	"
M. MEILLEUR, 32d,	"	"
G. MINIERI, 32d,	"	"
N. J. PEGRAM, 32d,	"	"
JOHN PEMBERTON, 32d,	"	"
C. RAYMOND, 32d,	"	"
D. I. RICARDO, 32d,	"	"
JUAN RICO, 32d,	"	"
S. G. RISK, 32d,	"	"
ALFRED SHAW, 32d,	"	"
JOHN C. SMITH, 32d,	"	"
A. TEXIER, 32d,	"	"
S. M. TODD, 32d,	"	"
B. P. VOORHIES, 32d,	"	"
R. WATSON, 32d,	"	"
J. C. WILNER, 32d.	"	"

MEMBERS OF THE GRAND CONSISTORY OF LOUISIANA.   39

FIFTH CLASS.

WILLIAM R. BELL, 32d,   Honorary Member.
JOHN CLAIBORNE, 32d,   "   "
S. G. FABIO, 32d,   "   "
J. C. GORDY, 32d,   "   "
JOSHUA JACKSON, 32d,   "   "
S. MEILLEUR, Sr., 32d,   "   "
B. DA SILVA, 32d,   "   "
WM. STEFFENS, 32d,   "   "
JOHN STRENNA, 32.   "   "

OFFICERS

OF THE

Grand Consistory of the State of Louisiana,

FOR THE YEAR 1857, V∴ E∴

ALBERT PIKE, 33d..........Ill∴, Commander-in-Chief.

L. H. PLACE, 33d.............Dep∴ Ill∴ Commander-in-Chief, *vice* Edw. [Barnett, resigned.

C. B. CLAPP, 33d.............First Lieutenant Commander.

F. A. LUMSDEN, 33d........Second Lieutenant Commander.

THOS. F. BRAGG, 33d.......G∴ Chanc∴, *vice* C. Laffon de Ladébat, [resigned.

A. SCHREIBER, 33d.........G∴ Treasurer.

J. Q. A. FELLOWS, 33d......G∴ M∴ of State.

C. WOLTERS, 33d.............G∴ Arch∴.

D. I. RICARDO, 32d..........G∴ Steward.

F. H. KNAPP, 33d............G∴ M∴ of Ceremonies.

JOHN GALPIN, 32d..........G∴ Standard Bearer.

J. H. HOLLAND, 33d........G∴ Captain of the Guards.

JUAN RICO, 32d.............G∴ Tyler.

C. RAYMOND, 32d............Assist∴ G∴ Tyler.

SUPREME COUNCIL
SOVEREIGN GRAND INSPECTORS GENERAL
THE ANCIENT AND ACCEPTED RITE,

For the Southern Jurisdiction of the United States.

FROM THE GRAND EAST OF CHARLESTON.

At a special session of this Supreme Council, holden in their Council Chamber, at the Grand East of Charleston near the B∴ B∴ and under the C∴ C∴, on the 23d day of the month "Sivan" A∴ M∴ 5617, corresponding to the 15th of June, A∴ L∴ 5857, it was ordered that the following balustre or proclamation be signed by the most Puissant Sovereign Grand Commander and the Illustrious Secretary General of the H∴ E∴, and that it be published for the information of all whom it may concern.

Extract from the records,

ALBERT G. MACKEY, M. D. 33d.

Secretary General.

AD UNIVERSI TERRARUM ORBIS SUMMI ARCHITECTI GLORIAM.

To all Illustrious Princes and Knights, Grand, Ineffable and Sublime Free Masons of all Degrees, ancient and modern, over the surface of the two Hemispheres to whom these presents shall come,

GREETING.

WHEREAS it has been made known to us that a body has lately been organized or attempted to be organized in the City of New Orleans,

2

calling itself the "*Supreme Council of Sov∴ Grand Inspectors General of the Ancient and Accepted Scotch Rite of the State of Louisiana*", whereof the following persons are declared to be officers and members, namely: James Foulhouze, G∴ C∴—T. Wharton Collens, L∴ G∴ C∴ — Louis Dufau, Sec∴ Gen∴ — Joseph Lisbony, G∴ Or∴ — J. B. Faget, G∴ Treas∴ and J. J. E. Massicot, G∴ C∴ of the G∴

NOW KNOW YE, that the Supreme Council for the Southern Jurisdiction of the United States deeming it derogatory to its dignity to repeat the many arguments and reasons by which it has, on former occasions, conclusively shown the illegality of any such organization in contravention of its acknowledged constitutional prerogatives and the Statutes and Regulations of the Rite, and which, for the last time, were most ably and unanswerably presented by our FAITHFUL and ILLUSTRIOUS Brother C. Samory, in the address delivered by him on the 15th day of February last before the Masons of New Orleans, will content itself by declaring, on the present occasion, that the so called "*Supreme Council of Louisiana*" of which James Foulhouze is represented as the Grand Commander, is but a new attempt to revive a claim long since abandoned, as being in direct violation of the CONSTITUTIONS OF 1786, which are the FUNDAMENTAL LAW of the Ancient and Accepted Rite. And the Supreme Council for the Southern Jurisdiction, in grand convention assembled, does hereby denounce the said "*Supreme Council of Louisiana*" of which James Foulhouze is represented as the Grand Commander, as SPURIOUS, ILLEGAL and CLANDESTINE; and it forbids all Masons under its own Jurisdiction and fraternally warns all Masons under every other Jurisdiction, from holding any masonic communication with the said SPURIOUS body, or with any councils, chapters or lodges which it may organize, under the most rigorous pains and penalties of disobedience.

And as a *spurious* and *irregular* organisation deficient, as this is, in all the elements of vitality, UNSUPPORTED by Constitutional Law and UNRECOGNIZED by ANY of the Supreme Councils of the World, can expect to prolong its existence only by the stimulus of an active and continued opposition, the Supreme Council for the Southern Jurisdiction requests and advises its Brethren of New Orleans especially, in the midst of whom this VISIONARY SCHEME has sprung forth, to enter into no arguments with its abettors, but to treat its organization and that of any subordinate bodies which it may establish, with that silent contempt which is justly due to so stupid an attempt to impair the peace and harmony of the Masonic Jurisdiction of Louisiana.

By Order of the Supreme Council,

JOHN H. HONOUR.
R∴ †∴, K–H∴, S∴ P∴ R∴ S∴, S∴ G∴ I∴ G∴, 33o,
M∴ P∴ S∴ G∴ Commander.

ALBERT G. MACKEY, M. D.
R∴ †∴, K–H∴, S∴ P∴ R∴ S∴, S∴ G∴ I∴ G∴, 33o,
Secretary General H∴ E∴

SEAL.

SPES MEA IN DEO EST.

AD UNIVERSI TERRARUM ORBIS SUMMI ARCHITECTI GLORIAM.

RESURGENS TENEBRAS VERA LUX DIMOVET.

Grand Consistory of S∴ PP∴ R∴ S∴, 32d D∴ of the Ancient and Accepted Scotch Rite in and for the State of Louisiana, under the Jurisdiction of the Supreme Council for the Southern Jurisdiction of the United States of America, sitting at Charleston, S. C.

WHEREAS, by advertisements published in the "New Orleans Bee," and in the "Picayune," of the 26th, 27th and 29th June, 1857, and to which the name of S. G. Fabin, 32d, is affixed as Secretary, a meeting is called of a certain body styling itself "Polar Star Chapter of Rose-Croix No. 3, under the jurisdiction of the SO-CALLED Supreme Council of Louisiana:

4

WHEREAS, the so-called *Supreme Council and Chapter* are SPU-RIOUS, IRREGULAR and CLANDESTINE Bodies, not recognized by any of the Masonic authorities of the Ancient and Accepted Scotch Rite in the U. S. A., or in any other part of the World :

WHEREAS, there exists in this Valley, under the Jurisdiction of this Grand Consistory, a chapter of Rose-Croix, bearing the same name and number as the SPURIOUS, ILLEGAL and CLANDESTINE Body above denounced :

AND WHEREAS, said *S. G. Fabio*, lately EXPELLED from this Grand Consistory, is no longer possessed of any Masonic qualification whatever:

NOTICE is hereby given to all whom it may concern, that the only REGULAR and LAWFUL Chapter of Rose-Croix, in this valley, bearing the name and number of POLAR STAR CHAPTER OF ROSE-CROIX No. 3, is that under the Jurisdiction of this Grand Consistory, and of which Ill∴ Bro∴ Charles Laffon de Ladébat, 33d, is M∴ W∴ and Ill∴ Bro∴ Michel Meilleur, 32d, Secretary.

Given under my hand and seal, at the Valley of New Orleans, this 7th day of "Tamuz," A∴ M∴ 5617—June 29th, 1857, V∴ E∴

L. H. PLACE, 33d,
Deputy Ill∴ Com∴ in chief
Grand Consistory of Louisiana.

By Order

THOS. F. BRAGG, 33d,
Grand Chancellor.

SPES MEA IN DEO EST.

AD UNIVERSI TERRARUM ORBIS SUMMI ARCHITECTI GLORIAM.

RESURGENS TENEBRAS VERA LUX DIMOVET.

Grand Consistory of S∴ PP∴ R∴ S∴, 32d D∴ of the Ancient and Accepted Rite in and for the State of Louisiana, under the Jurisdiction of the Supreme Council for the Southern Jurisdiction of the United States of America, sitting at Charleston, S. C.

Sitting of " Ab " 3d, A∴ M∴ 5617—July 24 1857, V∴ E∴.

WHEREAS, by advertisements in the " Bee " and in the " Picayune " of the 22d inst., this Grand Consistory is informed of the existence, in this Valley, of a certain body styling itself " Grand Council of Kadosh Polar Star No. 3," under the jurisdiction of a body assuming the title of Supreme Council for the Independent State of Louisiana ;

2

WHEREAS, the above so called *Grand Council and Supreme Council* are *clandestine, spurious* and *illegal* bodies, NOT RECOGNIZED BY ANY OF THE LEGAL AND LEGITIMATE MASONIC BODIES of the Ancient and Accepted Rite in either hemisphere;

And WHEREAS, there exists in this Valley A REGULAR AND LAWFUL COUNCIL OF KADOSH, bearing the same name and number as that assumed by the ILLEGAL AND SPURIOUS COUNCIL above denounced;

NOTICE is hereby given to all whom it may concern, that the only LEGAL and LAWFUL Council of Kadosh in this Valley, bearing the name and title of POLAR STAR COUNCIL OF KADOSH, No. 3, is that under the jurisdiction of this Grand Consistory, and of which Ill∴ Bro∴ C. Samory, 33d, is T∴ P∴ G∴ M∴, and Ill∴ Bro∴ Michel Meilleur, 33d, the Chancellor.

By order of the Grand Consistory :

[SEAL]

THOS. F. BRAGG, 33d,

G∴ Chancellor.

Lux e tenebris

www.ingramcontent.com/pod-product-compliance
Lightning Source LLC
Chambersburg PA
CBHW031513270326
41930CB00006B/399